D1882496

LAYS OF ANCIENT INDIA

Owing to the antiquity and rarity of this book, certain pages are regrettably absent, and readability is compromised due to the blurring of the original text. If you possess any insights regarding the availability of these missing sections, kindly inform us. Your assistance is crucial in ensuring the completion of this significant work for the benefit of future generations.

LAYS OF ANCIENT INDIA

ROMESH CHUNDER DUTT

GYAN

Published by

GYAN

Gyan Publishing House
5, Ansari Road
Daryaganj, New Delhi-110002
Phone: 011-47034999, 9811692060
E-mail: books@gyanbooks.com

Distribution Network
gyanbooks.com
India, USA, Canada, UK, Australia

© Publisher
All rights reserved. No part of this work may be reproduced, stored, adapted, or transmitted in any form or by any means, electronic, mechanical, photocopying, micro-filming, recording or otherwise, or translated in any language, without the prior written permission of the copyright owner and the publisher.

ISBN: 978-93-6780-439-1 (PB)

First Published, 1894

2nd Impression 2024

Printed at: Gyan Press, Delhi.

The book is sold subject to the condition that it shall not, by way of trade or otherwise, be lent, resold, hired out, or otherwise circulated without the prior publisher's written consent.

LAYS OF ANCIENT INDIA
Author: ROMESH CHUNDER DUTT

LAYS OF ANCIENT INDIA

SELECTIONS FROM
INDIAN POETRY RENDERED INTO
ENGLISH VERSE

BY

ROMESH CHUNDER DUTT, C.I.E.

BARRISTER-AT-LAW, AND OF THE INDIAN CIVIL SERVICE; MEMBER OF
THE ROYAL ASIATIC SOCIETY AND OF THE ASIATIC
SOCIETY OF BENGAL

AUTHOR OF "A HISTORY OF CIVILISATION IN ANCIENT INDIA," ETC.

LONDON
KEGAN PAUL, TRENCH, TRÜBNER, & CO. LTD
PATERNOSTER HOUSE, CHARING CROSS ROAD
1894

TO MY LOVING DAUGHTERS

AMALA AND SARALA

I

Dedicate this Volume

WITH

A FATHER'S BLESSING AND LOVE.

PREFACE

INDIAN poetry has been made known to English readers by distinguished English writers. A hundred years ago Sir William Jones translated the beautiful play of Sakuntalâ into English, and for the first time drew the attention of European readers to the beauty of Indian thought and poetry. H. H. Wilson followed in his footsteps, and rendered into graceful English verse some others of the best dramatic works in the Sanscrit language, and also a beautiful poem called Meghadûta. Wilson's English translation of the Rig Veda has since been completed and published; and Mr. Griffiths has brought out a commendable metrical translation of the great epic Râmâyana. Max Müller has translated the ancient Upanishads and the Buddhist work Dhammapada into English prose; and the genius of Sir Edwin Arnold has made thousands of readers in Europe and in America familiar with the wealth of Indian thought and imagery, and the beauty of Buddhist precepts and doctrines.

The time has come for placing before English readers a carefully prepared book of selections from the entire range of ancient Indian poetry. Such a book of selections should convey something not only of the beauty of Indian poetry in general, but also of the distinctive features of the poetry of each special period,—something of the freshness and simplicity of the Vedic Hymns, the sublime and lofty thought of the Upanishads, the unsurpassed beauty of Buddhist precepts, and the incomparable richness and imagery of the later or classical Sanscrit poetry. And it seems to me that such a book, comprising specimens from the literature of successive periods, is likely to give the English reader a general bird's-eye view of Indian poetry, Indian thought, and Indian religion.

I cannot help feeling my own unfitness for undertaking such a task in a language which is not my mother tongue. But nevertheless the reception which has been accorded to my work on *Civilisation in Ancient India* emboldens me to make the attempt; and I believe that the readers of my previous work, who have studied the history of ancient India through its successive periods, will feel some interest in the *Lays of Ancient India*, illustrating the life and thought of those periods.

The literature of ancient India, like its history, divides itself into five successive periods. The Vedic period is believed to cover five or six centuries, from 2000 to 1400 B.C.; and of the thousand hymns of the Rig Veda which have been left to us I have translated fourteen in the present volume. The freshness and joyousness of the Vedic Hymns characterise them as a true and faithful picture of the times in which they were composed.

The second or epic period is believed to cover four or five hundred years, from 1400 to about 1000 B.C. The great epics of India, the Mahâbhârata and the Râmâyana, were, in their original shape, composed in this period, and describe the deeds and wars of nations who lived in the Gangitic valley in this age. The Râmâyana has been rendered into English verse by Mr. Griffiths, and portions of the Mahâbhârata have been translated by eminent Englishmen, from Dean Milman to Sir Edwin Arnold. I have not attempted to do once more what these eminent writers have done. I have confined my selections of this period to those remarkable compositions, the Upanishads, which are among the most valuable works in the literatnre of the world. They show us how the Nature-worship of the Rig Veda developed itself into the worship of Nature's God,—the Universal Soul from whom the whole universe has emanated, and into whom the whole universe will resolve itself. This is the essence of the Hindu religion and of Hindu thought, and we find this thought in its purest and best form in the Upanishads. They are in prose, but breathe the sublimest poetry, and I have ventured to translate eight passages from these venerable works into English verse.

The third period is one of seven centuries, from 1000 B.C. to the time of Alexander the Great and Chandragupta of Magadha, about 320 B.C. Philosophy and science and grammar were cultivated with remarkable success in India in this period; and the ancient sacrificial rules and social and domestic rules were also compiled in compact works. And it was in this period that Gautama Buddha was born and preached that noble religion which is now the faith of a third of the human race. The Buddhist Scriptures belong to this age, and have been faithfully preserved in the Pali language in Ceylon. The life and teachings of the Light of Asia have been told in English verse as only a true poet can tell them, and there is no room for a mere translator to go over the same ground. I have therefore only given two passages from the Buddhist Scriptures, and a few maxims from the Dhammapada.

The fourth period covers about eight centuries, from B.C. 320 to about 500 A.D., and was the age when Buddhism prevailed in India side by side with the older creed of the Hindus. The imperial Asoka the Great ruled in this period, and issued those celebrated edicts which display to us, after the lapse of over two thousand years, his power, his greatness, and his righteousness. His edicts are of course in prose, but I have taken the liberty of translating two stirring passages from them into verse in the present volume. The Institutes of Manu, in their present shape, also belong to this period, but translations of these Institutes by Sir William Jones and by Bühler are available to the English reader.

The fifth and last epoch of ancient Indian history and literature covers some seven centuries, from about 500 to 1200 A.D. The voluminous Purânas were compiled in this age, which is therefore called the Puranic age; and what is known as the Kâvya poetry belongs to this age. The lovely creations of Kâlidâsa and Bhavabhûti and a host of other poets throw a brilliant light over the first three centuries of this period, and make the task of the translator a difficult and almost an impossible one.

A number of short epics, or Kâvyas, based mostly on the great ancient epics of India, were composed in this age; and these short epics are favourite subjects of study with the modern Hindus. They convey in fact the most perfect picture that we possess of Hindu thought, Hindu poetry, and even of Hindu religion in the later times, and no book of Indian poetry can pretend to be complete without a specimen of this kind of composition. I have therefore, after giving two passages from Kâlidâsa and one from Kshemendra, translated the entire story of a short epic by Bhâravi. And if this poem, The Hunter and the Hero, occupies a large portion of the present volume, it is because it represents a class of compositions which are a favourite study with the Hindus even to the present day, and convey the feelings, the ideas, and the popular beliefs of modern Hindus.

It is well known that the Indian drama is even richer than Indian poetry, but I have refrained in this volume from giving any specimens of the drama. In the first place, a play cannot be judged by extracts, and I cannot make room for entire plays. And in the second place, I could not render them as they have been rendered by the gifted H. H. Wilson. Indeed I shall consider my labours amply rewarded if the present volume can take a humble place by the side of Wilson's *Theatre of the Hindus.*

R. C. DUTT.

WIESBADEN, GERMANY,
August and September 1893.

CONTENTS

I. VEDIC HYMNS.

II. PASSAGES FROM THE UPANISHADS.

III. PASSAGES FROM BUDDHIST SCRIPTURES.

IV. EDICTS OF ASOKA.

V. KÂVYA POETRY.

VI. THE HUNTER AND THE HERO.

I.

VEDIC HYMNS.

"The Rig Veda consists of 1028 hymns, comprising over ten thousand verses. The hymns are generally simple, and betray a child-like and simple faith in the gods, to whom sacrifices are offered and libations of the Soma juice are poured, and who are asked for increase of progeny, cattle, and wealth, and implored to help the Aryans in their still doubtful struggle against the black aborigines of the Punjab."

—*Civilisation in Ancient India* (London, 1893), vol. i. p. 32.

INDRA, THE RAIN-GIVER.

"Vritra is supposed to confine the waters, and will not let them descend until the sky-god or rain-god, Indra, strikes the monster with his thunderbolt. The captive waters then descend in copious showers, rivers rise almost instantaneously, and gods and men rejoice over the changed face of nature."—*Civilisation in Ancient India*, vol. i. p. 79.

1.

I SING the lay, our fathers knew,—
How Indra mighty Vritra slew!
He pierced the rain-cloud in his might,
And gave us water, copious, bright!
The joyous mountain streams rolled swiftly by,
For Indra cleared for them the rocky way!

2.

He pierced the rain-cloud, stout of heart,
And Tvashtri forged the lightning's dart!
The grateful showers in torrents fell,
And joyous streamlets roar and swell!
And as the milch-kine hasten to their young,
Unto the sea the streamlets speed along!

3.

Impetuous like a bull in might,
Indra, eager for the fight,

Thrice drank the Soma;—in his hand
Grasped the forkéd lightning brand!
He pierced the foremost rain-cloud in his might,
And poured the joyous waters, sparkling bright!

4.

Mighty god and warrior proud!
You smote the demon of the cloud,
You quelled his power, destroyed his wile,
And cleared the earth from darkness vile!
Bright was the sky again with ruddy dawn,
And joyful mortals hailed the rising sun!

5.

In gloomy folds did Vritra proud
The earth and sky in darkness shroud
But with the lightning's fiery might
Great Indra pierced him in the fight!
Like a tall forest tree by woodmen felled,
Proud Vritra lies prostrate, by Indra killed!

6.

Did not Vritra, proud, elate,
Proudly challenge Indra great?
The mighty Indra, in his ire,
Has dealt on him his vengeance dire!
Splashing on the rivers Vritra fell,
How roar the whirling eddies, how they swell!

7.

With severed limbs, in mighty rage
The combat still did Vritra wage.
Once more the lightning flashed its fire,
On Vritra's neck fell in its ire.
The weak in vain will try the hero's might,
And vain was Vritra's war with Indra bright!

8.

Glad waters over Vritra roll,
As rivers over banks that fall.
Erst strong in might and strong in gloom,
He kept the waters in his womb.
How lies that demon, mighty in his fall!
Spurning the dead, how glad the waters roll!

9.

But darker clouds come in their might,
And Indra fights a fiercer fight!
Once more the forkéd lightnings fly,
Once more the clouds prostrated lie!
Low as a cow beside her calf is laid,
The mother rain-cloud lies with Vritra dead!

10.

O'er the dead the waters hie,
Sparkling as they ceaseless fly!

Low lies the nameless shapeless dead,
Bright roll the streams by torrents fed!
Then sing great Indra's praise with mighty breath,
For Indra's foe now sleeps the sleep of death!

11.

When light was prisoned by dark gloom,
'Twas Indra won her from its womb!
When rain was prisoned by the cloud,
'Twas Indra slew the demon proud!
Then sing great Indra's praise in mighty strain,
For Indra gave us light and gave us rain!

12.

Vain were Vritra's darts and blows,
For Indra shields himself from foes!
Vain was Pani's wily art,
The cows were won from Bilu's fort.*
Then sing great Indra's praise in mighty song,
He rolled the seven great rivers fierce and strong.†

* "The rays of light are compared to cattle which have been stolen by the powers of darkness, and *Indra* (the Sky) seeks for them in vain. He sends *Saramâ* (the Dawn) after them, and Saramâ finds out the *Bilu* or fortress where the *Panis* or powers of darkness have concealed the cattle. The Panis try to tempt Saramâ, but in vain. Saramâ comes back to Indra, and Indra marches with his forces, destroys the fort, and recovers the cattle; the darkness is gone, and it is day. . . . Professor Max Müller maintains that the story of the siege of Troy is a development of this simple Vedic myth. . . . Ilium, according to the Professor, is *Bilu*, the cave or the fortress of the Rig Veda. Paris is the Panis of the Veda who tempt, and Helena is the Vedic Saramâ who resists the temptation in the Veda, but succumbs to it in Greek mythology."—*Civilisation in Ancient India*, vol. i. p. 80.

† The Indus, its five tributaries, and the Sarasvati.

13.

The lightning shafts that Ahi * sent,
On Indra harmless all were spent;
And Ahi's thunders, gusts of rain,
Against the mighty god were vain!
And vain were Ahi's stratagems and arts,
For Indra rent them with his piercing darts!

14.

Great Indra! In that dubious war
Didst thou own a secret fear?
Did thy arm, for conquests made,
Await some other warrior's aid?
Or didst thou, like the swooping bird of prey,
O'er ninety streams and nine flee far away?

15.

Lightning-arméd! Mighty king
Of living and of lifeless thing!
The glorious monarch lives on high,
And sends us bright rain from the sky.
And as the spokes are circled by the rim,
Great Indra holds the universe in Him!

Rig Veda, I. 32.

* Another name of Vritra, or the rain-cloud.

INDRA, THE SUPREME DEITY.

I.

MORTALS! Did you question me,
Who is Indra, where is he?
He who is Celestial Light!
Leadeth gods and men in might!
He whose power pervades the earth and sky,
Mortals! He is Indra, rules on high!

2.

He who fixed the solid earth,
Shaped the mountains at their birth!
He whose mighty hand hath bent
The far extending firmament!
He who shaped the ever glorious sky,
Mortals! He is Indra, rules on high!

3.

He who pierced the clouds in might,
Rolled the seven great rivers bright!
He who quelled the demon gloom,
Conquered light from its dark womb!

He, in clouds who hurls the lightning bright,
Mortals! He is Indra, victor in the fight!

4.

Listen, mortals! to my verse,
His handiwork—this universe!
He has quelled the stubborn foe,
Banished him to live in woe!
He wrests the Dâsa's treasures from his hold,*
For he is Indra! hunter strong and bold!

5.

Have you, doubting, questioned me,
Where is Indra, who is he?
Mortals! In your impious thought
Have you whispered, He is not!
Dread the great punisher and his vengeance dire!
For Indra smites the impious in his ire!

6.

But his ceaseless mercies seek
The pious man, the poor and meek!
Gracious King! a crown he wears,
And listens to our hymns and prayers!
With grateful hearts libations pour to him,
For he is Indra, Lord of ancient fame!

* Indra is supposed to help the Aryan Hindu conquerors in their wars with the *Dâsas* or the aborigines of India.

7.

His the kine and steeds of war,
The village home, the battle car!
His arm lifts up the radiant sun,
And opes the ruddy gates of dawn!
His lightning shaft the darksome rain-cloud rends,
For he is Indra, copious rain who sends!

8.

Contending hosts repeat his name,
And chiefs invoke the Lord of fame!
Car-borne warriors shout his praise,
And trembling nations sing his praise!
Mortals! Unto him is worship due,
For he is Indra, whom our fathers knew!

9.

Man triumphs not but by his blade,
And warring nations ask his aid!
The universe he measures right,
And rolling worlds confess his might!
He sees th' eternal mountains wear away,
For Indra knows no death, no slow decay!

10.

He who killed with lightning dire
Impious nations in his ire;

He whoso blessings never rain
Upon the boastful and the vain;
He who crushed the Dâsas in his might,
He is Indra! victor in the fight!

11.

He who mighty warriors quelled,
In forty years Samvara felled;
He who struck the demon cloud,
Rent his vast and gloomy shroud;
He who strikes the impious in his might,
He is Indra! glorious in the fight!

12.

His seven bright tints bedeck the bow,
His seven great rivers joyous flow!
His lightning laid Rauhina low,
The heaven-aspiring, impious foe!
He who strikes the impious in his might,
He is Indra! conqueror in the fight!

13.

The earth and sky to Indra pray,
And trembling hills obeisance pay!
To Indra, wielder of the dart,
Libations pour and lift your heart!
The God of mighty strength and lightning hand,
He is Indra! wielder of the brand!

14.

Lift your heart and lift your praise,
Pour libations, chant his lays!
For hymns and gifts to him are dear,
And Indra guards us from all fear!
And he accepts our gifts and listens to our lays,
Mortals! He is Indra! Shout his praise!

15.

Great Indra! mortals raise thy song,
For thee their pious rites prolong,
From thee all gifts and blessings flow,
And thou art Truth! To thee we bow!
Grant us, great King! for bountiful thou art,
Sons, brave in war, and pious in their heart!

Rig Veda, II. 12.

VARUNA, GOD OF SKY.

"The eminent German scholar, Dr. Roth, is of opinion that before the Indo-Aryans and the Iranians separated, Varuna was the highest and holiest of the gods of their ancestors, and represented the spiritual side of their religion. After the separation had taken place, this deity of righteousness was translated in Iran into Ahura Mazd, the Supreme Deity. And although in India, Varuna yielded the foremost place among gods to the young and vigorous rain-giver, Indra, still he never became divested of that sanctity and holiness which entered into his first conception, and the holiest hymns of the Rig Veda are his, not Indra's."—*Civilisation in Ancient India*, vol. i. p. 76.

The first five verses of this hymn are addressed to the Fire and to the Sun, and are omitted in the translation.

1.

VARUNA, Lord of righteousness!
Thy wondrous power invites our lays!
The birds that sail across the sky,
Not with thy matchless speed can fly!
Nor the swift winds in their unceasing course,
Nor rapid torrents in resistless force!

2.

Glorious King of righteousness!
Thy seat is in ethereal space!
Thy radiance dwells in skies above,
And thence descends on us in love.
Mighty monarch of the upper sky!
Protect your humble worshippers from high!

3.

In heaven's expanse thy hand hath laid
The path for radiant sun to tread!
At thy command from morn till late
He treads the path so vast and great!
Destroy, O mighty King, the foeman's power,
And save, oh save us in the evil hour!

4.

Thine, the power to heal and bless!
Thine, deep wisdom, righteousness!
Keep us, Lord, from impious deeds,
From wicked thought that oft misleads.
Teach us, O King! the ways of vice to shun,
And save, oh save us from the sins we've done!

5.

Yon stars that spangle night's dark sky,*
In daylight whither do they flee?

* "The word used in the text is Riksha, which may either mean stars generally, or the stars of the constellation Great Bear. The root *rich* means to shine, whence in course of time the word Riksha came to have two meanings—the shining stars of a particular constellation, and an animal with bright eyes and shining glossy hair. By a natural confusion of ideas, therefore, the constellation itself ultimately came to be called the Bear. The question is discussed with remarkable eloquence and learning by Max Muller in his 'Science of Language,' and he explains that 'the surprise with which many a thoughtful observer has looked at these seven bright stars, wondering why they were ever called the Bear, is removed by reference to the early annals of human speech.'"—*Civilisation in Ancient India*, vol. i. p. 77.

These works, how glorious and how bright,
How strange, Varuna! is thy might!
The nightly stars thy mighty prowess own,
And thy behest obeys the shining moon!

6.

With pious hymns we sing thy praise,
We bring thee gifts, we chant thy lays!
In mercy listen unto me,
In mercy set the sinner free!
Nations speak thy mercy and thy power,
Then spare, oh spare me in this evil hour!

7.

My friends, they tell me, night and day,
My whispering heart doth ever say,—
Lift up to him thy holy lay
In trouble, turn to him and pray!
Your chains and fetters he will soon remove,*
For Varuna is mercy! He is love!

8.

Son of the Eternal Light! †
Remove my fetters in thy might!

* The poet Sunahsepa is supposed to be bound to the sacrificial post, and prays to Varuna to remove his chains and to pardon his sins.

† The word used in the text is Aditi, the parent of the bright gods. "Aditi means the undivided, the unlimited, the eternal. It is in reality, as has been stated, the earliest name invented by man to express the Infinite—the visible infinite, the endless expanse, beyond the

Sunahsepa prays to thee,
In mercy set the sinner free!
In boundless wisdom and resistless power,
Spare, oh spare me in this evil hour!

9.

Varuna of the righteous path!
By worship we assuage thy wrath;
Thy anger by our gifts remove,
Relent in mercy and in love!
Accept the sacrifice we have begun,
Remove the fetters of the sins we've done!

10.

Remove the fetters from above,
The middle chains, O Lord, remove,
Remove the galling chains below,
And let me to thy mercy bow!
Son of Eternal Light! let me remain
Obedient to thy laws and free from sin!

Rig Veda, I. 24.

earth, beyond the clouds, beyond the sky. . . . It means, according to the eminent German scholar, Dr. Roth, the eternal and inviolable principle, the celestial light."—*Civilisation in Ancient India*, vol. i. p. 83.

VARUNA, THE GOD OF RIGHTEOUSNESS.

1.

IN boundless radiance is his birth,
He holds the spacious sky and earth,
The heaven's blue vault he lifts on high,
And spreads the stars across the sky!
And the broad earth, so boundless and so grand,
It is the work, Varuna! of thy hand!

2.

Shall I with my humble prayer
Before this mighty God appear?
Will he in his mercy take
The gifts a mortal dares to make?
With mind from sins and impure passions free,
Oh when shall I his radiant visage see?

3.

With anxious thought to thee I turn,
Teach me, Lord! that I may learn,
What mighty sin pollutes my heart,
And racks me with a cruel smart?
I've questioned men of lore to know the way,
And they have told me, Lord! to turn to thee!

4.

Teach me, Lord! what sin unknown
Hath its shadow o'er me thrown?
Wilt thou in thy anger smite
Thy worshipper, O Lord of light?
Teach me, Lord! to expiate my sin,
Teach me, Lord! to turn to thee again!

5.

Gracious Monarch! make us freed
From the sins our fathers did;
Help to expiate and shun
Unholy acts that we have done!
Like tethered cattle, or like trembling thief,
I tremble, Lord! But thou canst save my life!

6.

Error often leads to sin,
Wine and anger lead to ruin,
Dice and gambling to distress,
And folly to unrighteousness!
The elder oft the younger will mislead,
And even our dreams unholy thoughts will breed!

7.

Then save me, Lord! for thou canst save,
Protect thy worshipper, thy slave.

Freed from sin, and strong in mind,
I'll serve Varuna, ever kind!
Grant us, Aryan * God! light on our path,
And grant us strength, for we are weak in faith!

8.

Accept, Varuna! in thy grace,
These humble but these pious lays,
And may it ever pleasing be
The hymn we humbly sing to thee!
And may thy worshippers, with virtue blest,
Find bliss in everything, and peace and rest!

Rig Veda, VII. 86.

* *Devo Aryo* in the original text.

AGNI, OR THE FIRE.

"Agni is the god of Fire; the Ignis of the Latins, the Ogni of the Sclavonians."—Muir's *Sanscrit Texts.*

"All the names of the Fire and the Fire-gods were carried away by the Western Aryans; and we have Prometheus answering to Pramantha, Phoronus to Bharanyu, and the Latin Vulcanus to the Sanscrit Ulka." —Cox's *Mythology of Aryan Nations.*

The hymn translated below is one of peculiar interest, because it is said to have been composed by a pious lady, Visvavârâ.

1.

LIGHTED Agni flames forth high,
Flings a radiance on the sky,
And his lustre, glorious, bright,
Mingles with the morning light.
And Visvavârâ chants her holy prayer,
Faces the east, and brings her gifts to Fire!

2.

Lord of Eternity! Lord of skies!
Presiding Lord of sacrifice!
Agni! Whoso worships thee,
By him with thy blessings be!
Whose blazing altar sacred Agni lights,—
Affluence dwells with him and pious rites.

3.

Agni! On the altar shine,
Flames and radiance bright be thine!
Grant us wealth with thy red flame,
Quell our foes, increase our fame!
Invest our homes with blessings from above,
And link our men and wives in bonds of love!

4.

Agni! On the altar shine,
Flames and radiance bright be thine!
And I lift my pious hymn
To thy bright effulgent beam!
Bounteous god! Red lustre e'er be thine,
Flame on our altar, glorious and divine!

5.

With pious hands we light thy flame,
With pious lips we chant thy name!
Invoke unto our sacrifice
The glorious bright gods of the skies!
For thou art Priest* in every pious rite,
And makest gifts to gods with radiance bright!

* "As no sacrifice could be performed without fire, Agni, or Fire, was called the invoker of the gods."—*Civilisation in Ancient India*, vol. i. p. 85.

6.

Then let us unto Agni pray,
And he our offerings will convey!
And let us unto Agni sing,
And he the radiant gods will bring!
Priest and God! to thee we humbly pray,
Our pious offerings to the gods convey!

Rig Veda, V. 28.

USHAS, OR THE DAWN.

"There is no lovelier conception in the Rig Veda than that of the Dawn. There are no hymns in the Veda more truly poetical than those dedicated to her, and nothing more charming is to be found in the lyrical poetry of any ancient nation. . . . The Dawn was known by various names, and most of these names, and the legends connected with them, were brought by the Hindus from their original abode, since we find phonetical equivalents of these names, and a repetition of some of the legends too, in Greek mythology. Ushas is the Eos of the Greeks and the Aurora of the Latins. Arjunî, according to philologists, is the Greek Argynoris, Brisayâ is Briseis, and Dahanâ is Daphne. Saramâ is phonetically equivalent to the Greek Helena. Saranyu, the mother of Yama and of the Asvins, is the Greek Erinys, and Ahanâ is the renowned goddess Athena."—*Civilisation in Ancient India*, vol. i. p. 91.

1.

BEAUTEOUS daughter of the sky!
Hold thy ruddy light on high!
Grant us wealth and grant us day,
Bring us food with morning's ray!
White-robed goddess of the morning sky!
Bring us light,—let night's deep shadows fly!

2.

Rich in cattle, rich in steed,
With thy gifts to mortals speed!

Joyous nations welcome thee,
For thy gifts are ever free.
Speak, goddess! words of comfort and of joy,
And grant us wealth and bliss without alloy.

3.

Our fathers hailed thy glorious light,—
We hail thee, goddess, ever bright!
Like ships by merchants sent to sea,
Thy radiant chariot bringeth thee!
Come then, goddess! in thy glittering car,
Come and bring thy joyous light from far!

4.

And men of lore will raise their song,
The morning hymns to thee belong!
Kanva sings his pious lays
To thy soft resplendent rays.
Kanva, wisest of the men of lore,
Proclaims their names who feed and bless the poor!*

5.

Come like a housewife gentle-hearted,
Tending all!—For night's departed.

* Kanva is a Vedic poet. His son is supposed to have composed this hymn. The practice of repeating the names of holy and charitable men early in the morning still obtains in India.

Grant another joyous day
To beasts that walk and birds that fly.
And men and beasts will to their work repair,
And birds with joyous notes will fill the air!

6.

The strong man to his work you send,
Unto the poor your favours lend;
Soft is thy fresh and ruddy ray,
And ah! too fleeting is thy stay!
Hasten, then, and we to work repair,
And birds with joyous notes will fill the air!

7.

She comes! she comes! in her bright car
Scattering splendour from afar!
From regions far above the sun
In hundred chariots comes the Dawn!
She comes! she comes! in radiant loveliness,
She comes! she comes! to heal us and to bless!

8.

Mortals in devotion bend,
Hymns and shouts of joy they send!
For she comes with ruddy rays,
And she comes to heal and bless!
She brings us gifts in her resplendent car,
Removes our wants and drives our foes afar!

9.

Beauteous daughter of the sky!
Spread thy ruddy light on high!
Day by day, in morning bright,
Bring us blessings with your light!
Bring us gifts in thy resplendent car,
And drive the shades of gloomy night afar!

10.

Ruddy daughter of the sky!
Our life, our work, is all in thee!
For thou dispell'st the gloomy night,
And thou art day, resplendent bright!
Thou hear'st our hymns and prayers from afar,
And bring'st us gifts in thy resplendent car!

11.

White-robed daughter of the sky!
Our wine and cakes we offer thee!
Our joyous hymns to thee ascend,
To thee in worship mortals bend.
Grant that their pious rites from harm be free,
Grant that their pious hearts may turn to thee!

12.

Glorious daughter of the sky!
Bring with thee the gods from high!

Grant us milch-kine, grant us steed,
And our rites with blessings speed!
Grant us food and wealth and mighty name,
Grant us strength and health and warrior's fame!

13.

Blushing daughter of the sky!
Spread thy radiance far and nigh!
Vanquish foemen in the fight,
Perish all their power and might!
Grant us, radiant goddess! food and health,
Grant us strength in arms and copious wealth.

14.

Gracious daughter of the sky!
Our fathers in the days gone by
For thy blessings ever prayed,
For thy gifts, auspicious maid!
And we too lift our hearts and hymns to thee,
Accept our joyous songs and pious lay!

15.

Wide ope the portals of the sky!
Light comes in and shadows fly!
Wide and far thy blessings shower,
Save us with thy healing power!
Wide be our homes and free from harm and woe,
Rich be our flocks, our crops in plenty grow!

16.

Nymph of radiant loveliness!
Grant us food and grant us bliss!
Grant us cattle, wealth and fame,
And a warrior's mighty name!
Grant us, goddess! safety from all woe,
For thou art good,—from thee all blessings flow!

Rig Veda, I. 48.

SAVITRI, OR THE SUN.

"Sûrya and Savitri are the most common names of the sun in the Rig Veda, the former word answering to the Greek Helios, the Latin Sol, and the Iranian Khorshed. Commentators draw a distinction between Savitri, the rising or the unrisen sun, and Sûrya, the bright sun of the day."—*Civilisation in Ancient India*, vol. i. p. 84.

The following three verses are taken from a somewhat long hymn. The first of these verses is the famous *Gayatri*, the morning prayer of the Brâhmans. It has a deep significance, and pious worshippers in invoking the sun invoke the Higher Power whose radiance and glory are outwardly manifested in the sun.

1.

SAVITRI! effulgent, bright!
Who fosters every pious rite,
Savitri! whose ruddy rays
Invite our holy hymns and lays,
With humble hearts we contemplate his rays,
And faintly see our God in his bright face!

2.

Savitri will bring us food,
And Bhaga, bounteous and good.*

* "There is much confusion in the Rig Veda as to who the Âdityas are—the sons of this Celestial Light (Aditi). In II. 27, Aryaman and Bhaga and Daksha and Ansa are named, besides Varuna and Mitra. . . . When in course of time the year was divided into twelve months, the number of the Âdityas was fixed at twelve, and they were the suns of the twelve months."—*Civilisation in Ancient India*, vol. i. pp. 83, 84.

Savitri will hear our lays,
And Bhaga listens to our praise.
The radiant gods will bring us food and wealth,
And shield us from all harm, and grant us health.

3.

Let our pious men of lore
In our rites libations pour,
Let them in their wisdom raise
Holy hymns and songs of praise
For Savitri! Our god, our friend thou art!
And we will greet thee with a pious heart!

Rig Veda, III. 62.

THE GODS OF AGRICULTURE.

I.

KSHETRAPATI! Ever dear,*
With thee, we to fields repair!
We will till the grateful field,
Copious harvests it will yield!
Well fed and strong our bullocks and our steeds,
And Kshetrapati will supply our needs.

2.

Copious milk our cows supply,
And Kshetrapati, from the sky,
Sends us copious, grateful rain,
Sweet to tillers of the plain!
Sing to the god of tillage, ever dear,
He grants us crops and listens to our prayer!

3.

May our crops in sweetness grow,
In sweetness may the waters flow.

* *Kshetrapati* literally means the Lord of the field.

Kshetrapati! power divine!
Grace and sweetness, they are thine!
With grateful songs and hearts we follow thee,
And let our homes and fields from harm be free!

4.

Gladly works the merry swain,
And glad the mighty bullocks strain;
Gladly o'er the yielding soil
The shining ploughshare marks their toil!
Merrily fasten all the traces strong,
Merrily ply the goad and drive along!

5.

Let us raise our grateful song
To Suna, Sîra, bright and strong.*
Ye are gods to tillers dear,
Listen to their humble prayer!
And the bright rain you store within the sky
Will feed the grateful earth as crops grow high!

6.

Auspicious Sitâ! beauteous born!
Goddess of the shining corn!

* Sira and Suna are gods of agriculture,—the Sun and Air according to Yâska.

Listen to our grateful lays,
Grant to us thy helpful grace!
Grant us, Sîtâ! wealth and happiness,
Grant us, goddess! plenteous crops and bliss.*

7.

Indra takes her by the hand,
Pûshan leads her o'er the land,
From the sky obedient drops,
At her bidding feed our crops,
And as the harvest cometh year by year,
With plenteous crops, O goddess! still appear!

8.

The merry ploughshare marks the plain,
And merry work the beasts and men!
And Parjanya, the god of rain,
With grateful showers will feed the plain!
Then raise your pious hearts and grateful song
To Suna and to Sîra, bright and strong!

Rig Veda, IV. 57.

* "The furrow, Sitâ, is addressed as a female, and asked to yield copious harvests. In the Yajur Veda also, the furrow is similarly worshipped. And when the Aryans gradually conquered the whole of India, and primeval jungles and waste lands were marked with the furrow, the furrow, or Sitâ, assumed a more definite human character, and became the heroine of the Epic which describes the Aryan conquest of Southern India."—*Civilisation in Ancient India*, vol. i. pp. 35, 36.

THE GOD OF PASTURE.

"Pûshan is the sun as viewed by shepherds in their wanderings in quest of fresh pasture-lands. He travels in a chariot yoked with goats, guides men and cattle in their travels and migrations, and knows and protects the flocks. The hymns to Pûshan, therefore, often breathe a simplicity which is truly pastoral."—*Civilisation in Ancient India*, vol. i. pp. 84, 85.

1.

PÛSHAN ! radiant god of day !
Lead us o'er the dangerous way.
Vanquish every hurtful foe,
Free our path from every woe,
Child of the Clouds ! Oh lead us evermore,—
We follow,—as our fathers did before !

2.

Smite the skulking robber vile,
Lurking in the dark defile ;
Smite the murderer and the thief
Who wait in stealth to take our life.
Remove the wily foes who lurk before,
And Pûshan ! lead us safe for evermore ! *

* The third and fourth verses are almost a repetition of what precedes, and have been omitted in the translation.

3.

Thou the pathless waste dost know,
And Pûshan! thou canst quell the foe!
Thou didst lead our fathers right
In their wanderings, Pûshan bright!
Then lead us, radiant god! for evermore,—
We follow,—as our fathers did before!

4.

And thou hast treasures manifold,
Radiant weapons, arms of gold,
Foremost of the sons of light,
Bounteous leader, Pûshan bright!
Grant us wealth from thy unfailing store,
And we will praise thy bounty evermore!

5.

Lead us safely in thy might,
Where the wily foemen wait;
Lead us over pleasant ways,
Help us with thy bounteous grace.
Oh! lead us, Pûshan, in this trackless shore,
And lead us, radiant god! for evermore!

6.

Where the grass is rich and green,
Where the pasture's beauteous seen,

Lead us o'er such pleasant way,
Chase all ills and woes away!
Oh! lead us, Pûshan! in this trackless shore,
And lead us, radiant god! for evermore!

7.

Grant us blessings rich and good,
Fill our homes with plenteous food;
Grant us pastures far and near,
Make us, Pûshan! strong in war!
Oh! lead us, Pûshan! in this trackless shore,
And lead us, radiant god! for evermore!

8.

We lift our hearts and sing his praise,
To Pûshan chant our pious lays,
And from the good and gracious god
We ask for wealth and ask for food.
Oh! lead us, Pûshan! in this trackless shore,
And lead us, radiant god! for evermore!

Rig Veda, I. 42.

A BATTLE HYMN.

"Sudâs was an Aryan king and conqueror, and we are frequently told that various Aryan tribes and kings combined against him, and he was victorious over them all. The allusions to these internecine wars among Aryan races, and to the particular tribes who fought against Sudâs, are historically among the most important passages in the Rig Veda. . . . The poet Tritsu or Vasishtha, who sang these deeds of Sudâs's glory, was not unrewarded for his immortal verse. For in verses 22 and 23 (Hymn VII. 18) he acknowledges with gratitude that the valiant Sudâs rewarded him with two hundred cows and two chariots and four horses with gold trappings."—*Civilisation in Ancient India*, vol. i. p. 55.

1.

VARUNA glorious! Indra bright!
Our troops have eastward marched to fight.
Shining javelins in their hand,
They'll conquer cattle, conquer land!
Quell mighty gods, the Dâsa and the foe,
And save our King Sudâs from every woe!

2.

When mustered nations lift on high
Their banners floating in the sky,
When warriors anxious lift their gaze
From reddened field to sky's dark haze,
Ye mighty gods! be then our hope and stay,
And help our King Sudâs in dubious fray!

3.

When to the bewildered eye
The broad earth mingles with the sky,
When the deafening shouts arise
And assail the echoing skies,
And when the foeman's marshalled troops appear,
Then save our King Sudâs, and be ye near!

4.

Gods auspicious! you have quelled
The mighty foe, yet unassailed;—
You have been Sudâs's stay,
Helped him in the dubious fray!
And you have heard the Tritsus' holy lay,
Their priestly work bore fruit in battle's day!

5.

Our foemen in the battle's day,
Strong and stubborn in the fray,
Adept in all the warlike arts,
Pierced us with their countless darts.
Ye mighty gods! to you we raised our lay,
And you have helped our King, and were our stay.

6.

Our foemen called on you in vain,
Ye listen not to impious men!

In vain they sigh for wealth and lands,
For impious hearts make feeble hands!
Ten hostile kings, combined, their troops did bring;
Ye heard the Tritsus! Saved Sudâs, our king!

7.

Ten kings who know no pious rite
Did in vain their troops unite!
In vain did they their weapons bring
Against Sudâs, our mighty king!
You listened to the Tritsus' holy lay,
For gods accord their help when mortals pray!

8.

With their long and braided hair
Tritsu's white-robed sons appear,
And with pious gifts and song
The holy sacrifice prolong!
Ten hostile kings attacked our monarch brave!
In vain! the gods were nigh, and they can save!

9.

Indra slays the foe in fight,
Varuna tends our pious rite!
For your glory, for your praise,
We will chant our pious lays!
Ever gracious to the voice of prayer,
Bounteous gods! to worshippers appear!

10.

Varuna! Indra! strong in might,
Aryaman! and Mitra bright!
Grant to us, ye sons of light,
A home and all your favours bright.
Be good to us, Aditi's holy ray,
And we will chant Savitri's glorious lay!

Rig Veda, VII. 83.

A BRIDAL HYMN.

The last six verses of this long hymn have been translated. They are a part of the marriage ritual of the ancient times, and will interest modern readers.

1.

[*To the Bride and Bridegroom :*]

HAPPY man and beauteous bride!
Be this place your home of pride,
Loving man and duteous wife!
In peaceful union pass your life.
May prattling children fill your home with peace,
And lisping babes their grandsire's bliss increase!

2.

[*The Bride and Bridegroom say :*]

The Lord on us his gifts bestow,
And happy children round us grow!
In peaceful union pass our life,
Loving man and duteous wife!

[*To the Bride :*]

In thy new home auspicious life be thine!
Be good unto our men and to our kine!

3.

[*To the Bride:*]

Serve thy lord with love and sweetness,
Be thy soft eyes full of brightness,
Be thy beauty ever bright,
Be thy temper ever sweet!
Bear warlike sons! and worship gods divine!
Be good unto our men and to our kine!

4.

[*Prayer to Indra:*]

In thy mercy, in thy grace,
Grant her wealth and happiness!
A duteous housewife in her love,
May she happy mother prove!
And may ten warlike sons to her be born,
And from her spouse her heart may never turn!

5.

[*To the Bride:*]

A gentle kindness ever bear
To your husband's parents dear;
Bring within your loving rule
His sisters and his brothers all;
With queenly grace extend your gentle reign,
Be good unto our cattle and to men!

6.

[*The Bride and Bridegroom say:*]

All the gods who live above
May they blend our hearts in love,
May each bright celestial power
Bless us in this nuptial hour!
May they link us in a holy bliss,
And fill our peaceful home with happiness!

Rig Veda, X. 85.

A FUNERAL HYMN.

"There are some reasons, which Professor Max Müller explains with his usual eloquence, for supposing that the original conception of Yama in the Rig Veda is the conception of the departing sun. The sun sets and disappears, just as a man's life ends; and the imagination of a simple race would easily conjure up an after-world where that departed deity would preside over departed spirits. . . . In the Veda, he is the beneficent king of the happy world where the virtuous live and enjoy themselves in after-life. Clothed in a glorious body, they sit by the side of Yama in the realms of light and sparkling waters, they enjoy endless felicity there, and are adored here below under the name of Pitris, or fathers."—*Civilisation in Ancient India*, vol. i. p. 87.

The following hymn is a part of the funeral ritual of ancient times, and will be read with interest.

1.

AWAKE the song, the offerings bring,
To mighty Yama, gracious king!
For he has cleared for us the way
To realms of bliss and light of day!
And pious souls to Yama take their flight,
To realms of sparkling waters and of light!

2.

Yama showed to us the way!
The path that never fades away!
Our fathers by that path have gone
To the realms of setting sun!

And every being, after life's brief day,
Shall travel by the same eternal way! *

3.

Then come thou, Yama! gracious King,
And with thee our forefathers bring!
The feast we spread, the hymns we sing,
Then consecrate these rites, O King!
Pleased with our gifts, partake our ample feast,
And with our fathers in this mansion rest!

4.

Then come thou, Yama! gracious King,
And with thee our forefathers † bring!
Vivasvat, thy mighty sire,
Comes he to our sacred fire!
On the soft and sacred *varhis* ‡ rest,
Pleased with our gifts, partake our ample feast!

5.

The Angirasas, Bhrigus great,
And Atharvans § on us wait!
From the regions of the blest
Come to share our ample feast!
Then pour libations to our fathers great,
And may our rites their approbation meet!

* One verse after this has been omitted. It is full of proper names and obscure allusions.

† *I.e.*, the Angirasas, a celebrated priestly house.

‡ Sacrificial grass.

§ All celebrated ancient priestly houses.

6.

[*To the Dead Person:*]

By the path our fathers know,
Go, departed being! go!
In realms where sparkling rivers roll,
Live, and happy be thy soul!
Varuna great, and Yama, gracious king,
Dwell in these realms, then hasten on thy wing!

7.

Haste thee on thy unseen wing,
Flee to Yama, gracious king!
Meet our fathers who have gone,
Reap the virtues you have won!
Leave sins behind,—follow the setting sun,
Leave mortal shape,—a brighter form put on! *

Rig Veda, X. 14.

* There are eight more verses in the original, which have not been translated.

THE GOLDEN CHILD.

The following is one of the hymns of the Rig Veda which show that the mind of the ancient Hindu worshipper travelled "from Nature up to Nature's God."

1.

To whom in earth or sky or air
Shall we offer gifts and prayer?
To Him, the Golden Child, the One,
Existent from creation's dawn!
To Him who built the earth and spread the sky,
We bring our offerings, chant our prayers high!

2.

To whom in earth or sky or air
Shall we offer gifts and prayer?
To Him who lighted life's first ray,
Whose will celestial hosts obey!
Whose mighty shade is immortality!
Whose slave is death! Transcendent Deity!

3.

To whom on earth or sky or air
Shall we offer gifts and prayer?

To Him, the glorious King, above,
Of living things that see and move!
The Lord of men and beasts, of birds in air,
To Him we offer gifts and chanted prayer!

4.

To whom in earth or sky or air
Shall we offer gifts and prayer?
To Him whose mighty hand hath made
The earth's broad fields, the ocean's bed,
The snowy mountains, the far-spreading sky,
To Him we lift our prayers chanted high!

5.

To whom in earth or sky or air
Shall we offer gifts and prayer?
To Him who fixed the earth and sky,
And spread the glorious heavens on high,
The highest heaven whose fingers fixed and bent,
Whose hand has measured out the firmament!

6.

To whom in earth or sky or air
Shall we offer gifts and prayer?
Who hung the sky at nature's birth
And spread this broad and spacious earth!
The sounding sky and earth each shining hour,
And radiant sun attest His mighty power!

7.

To whom in earth or sky or air
Shall we offer gifts and prayer?
To Him,—the Life of gods!—the One!
Who breathed forth at creation's dawn!
When mighty waters filled chaotic gloom,
And held the nascent *agni* in their womb.*

8.

To whom in earth or sky or air
Shall we offer gifts and prayer?
Who held the waters in the gloom,
And breathed forth life into their womb,
To Him, the God of gods, the mighty One!
Who held the universe at creation's dawn!

9.

To whom in earth or sky or air
Shall we offer gifts and prayer?
To Him, the earth and sky who made,
And the mighty waters laid,
For He is Truth! the great Almighty Power!
And He will save us in the evil hour!

* The Hindu scriptures, like those of other nations, hold that in the beginning water pervaded the universe.

10.

Lord of Universe and King!
Thy hand hath shaped each living thing!
To Thee we lift our humble praise,
For Thou canst save, and Thou canst bless!
Fulfil our wishes, bless our sacrifice,
And on Thy worshippers bestow Thy grace!

Rig Veda, X. 121.

THE CREATOR.

This hymn consists of nine verses. Only the first three are given below in translation. They explain the sublime idea that all the different gods are only the different names of the One God, that all the powers of Nature are the manifestations of the One Power.

I.

OUR Father at creation's birth
Made the sky and made the earth,
The broad earth mingled with the sky,
In watery form they both did lie.
His mighty hand the heavens then lifted high,
And stretched the limits of the earth and sky.

2.

The All-Creator, He is great,
He shaped all things in every state,
Above all creatures,—mighty King,—
He sees and holds up everything.
Higher than where the stars of Great Bear shine,—
Great King of all!—a loftier seat is Thine!

3.

He our Father! He our King!
Whose hand created everything,
Whose world-pervading eye surveys
The world's far limits,—ends of space!
The names of many gods and powers He bears,
But He is One! To Him ascend our prayers!

Rig Veda, X. 82.

II.

PASSAGES FROM THE UPANISHADS.

"Who can, even in the present day, peruse these pious inquiries and fervent thoughts of a long buried past without feeling a new emotion in his heart, without seeing a new light before his eyes? The mysteries of the unknown future will never be solved by human intellect or by human science; but the first recorded attempts to solve them in a pious, fervent, philosophical spirit will ever have an abiding interest for every patriotic Hindu and for every thoughtful man.

"In the words of the eminent German writer and philosopher, Schopenhauer: 'From every sentence, deep, original, and sublime thoughts arise, and the whole is pervaded by a high and holy and earnest spirit. Indian air surrounds us, and original thoughts of kindred spirits. . . . In the whole world there is no study except that of the originals, so beneficial and so elevating as that of the Oupnekhat.* It has been the solace of my life; it will be the solace of my death.'"

—*Civilisation in Ancient India*, vol. i. p. 198.

* Latin translation of the Upanishads.

BRAHMAN, OR THE UNIVERSAL SOUL.*

"The monotheism of the Upanishads, which has been the monotheism of the Hindu religion ever since, recognises God as the Universal Being; all things else have emanated from Him, are a part of Him, and will mingle with Him."—*Civilisation in Ancient India*, vol. i. p. 191.

1.

THIS Universe is Brahman's Self!
A part of Him,—these creatures all!
In Him their birth, they live in Him,
And into Him they end withal!
The mortal ever toils and works,
And as he sows upon this earth,
In virtue's soil or ways of sin,
So reaps he in a future birth!

2.

He is Life,—Intelligence pure!
He is Truth and He is Light!
His soul pervades the universe,
Like ether,—escapes our mortal sight!

* It is necessary perhaps to note for our readers' information that Brahman with a short *a* means the Universal Being, and Brâhman with a long *â* is a worshipper of that Being, *i.e.*, a man of the priestly caste.

From Him alone all works proceed,
All wishes and all feelings spring,
Serene and calm, He never speaks,
But in Himself holds everything!

3.

He is the Self within my heart,
The Soul that lives and dwells within,
Smaller than the smallest seed,
Or kernel of smallest grain!
He is the Self within my heart,
Greater than the earth and sky,
Greater far than all the worlds,
Greater than the heaven on high!

4.

From Him alone all works proceed,
All wishes and all feelings spring,
Serene and calm, He never speaks,
But in Himself holds everything!
He is the Self within my heart,
He is Brahman!—holding all,
And when I leave this world,—to Him
Will flee my liberated soul!

Chhândogya Upanishad, III. 14.

THE LEGEND OF SATYAKÂMA.

I.

SATYAKÂMA,—truthful boy,—
Poor Jabâlâ's humble son,
Felt a passion in his soul
For the truth and truth alone!
So he came unto his mother,
Asked her of his father's name,
"Mother! I would be a student,
Tell me of what race I am."

2.

Jabâlâ the humble woman
Spoke in grief but spoke the truth,
"Sinfully I long have wandered,
And conceived thee in my youth!
And I know not who thy father,
Know not of what race thou art,
By the name of thy poor mother
Call thyself, child of my heart!"

3.

Satyakâma,—truthful boy,—
To Gautama went the youth,
"I would be a student, Sir,
For I seek to know the truth."
Gautama a welcome gave
To the boy who to him came,
"Tell me of what race thou art,
Tell me what may be thy name."

4.

Satyakâma,—truthful boy,—
Spoke in grief but spoke the truth,
"Sinfully my mother wandered,
And conceived me in her youth.
And I know not who my father,
Know not of what race I am,
Jabâlâ is my poor mother,
Jabâlâ must be my name."

5.

"Enough, enough, my truthful boy,"—
Spake the sage unto the youth,—
"By your worth you are a Brâhman,
For you dare to speak the truth!
Go and fetch the sacred fuel,
I will teach you, noble youth,
In the learning of our fathers,
For you have not swerved from truth!"

6.

Satyakâma brought the fuel,*
Was a student young and brave,
And he kept his teacher's cattle,
Served his teacher as his slave.
And unto the pathless meadows
With the cattle went the youth,
In his high and eager bosom
Nature flashed the light of truth!

7.

From the strong and noble bull
Of the herd that he was tending,
From the evening's faggot fire
Over which he pondered bending,
From the gay and bright flamingo
As it sailed across the sky,
From the diver-bird so beauteous
Which unto him was not shy,

8.

From the anxious contemplation
Which for ever filled his mind,
When the evening fire was lighted
And the cattle had been penned,

* The fuel is required for the rite of *initiating* a boy in the Vedas and the sacred learning of old.

From each humble, lowly object,
  Came its meaning to the youth,
From great Nature's mighty wonders
  Flashed on him the light of truth!

9.

And to Gautama he came,
  And a light was on his face!
For a knowledge of the truth
  Flings its glamour and its grace!
"Lo! a light is on thy face,
  Dost thou know the mighty Brahman?
Only those who know the Brahman
  With such light and radiance shine?"

10.

"Father! I have sought to know,"—
  Sweetly answered thus the youth,—
"Not from men I gathered knowledge,
  Nature whispered to me truth!
The earth, the quarters of the sky,
  The lofty heavens, the ocean broad,
The sun and moon, the mind and soul,—
  All, all is Brahman,—all is God!"

Abridged from Chhândogya Upanishad, IV. 4.

THE LEGEND OF GÂRGÎ.

I.

JANAKA, the holy monarch,
  Erst in wide Videha * reigned,
Made a mighty sacrifice,
  And an ample feast ordained!
Brâhmans from the Kuru kingdom
  And from broad Panchâla † came,
For they knew Janaka's bounty,
  And they heard Janaka's fame.

2.

Who of these assembled Brâhmans,
  To the sacrifice who came,
Is the wisest,—deepest learnéd,
  Worthiest of a Brâhman's name?
Such the thought that stirred the bosom
  Of Janaka, monarch bold,
And he penned a thousand milch kine,
  On each horn was hung some gold!

* Tirhoot, or North Behar.

† The Panchâla kingdom extended along the Ganges, round about the site of modern Kanouj. The Kuru kingdom extended higher up the same river, and also westwards, including the site of modern Delhi. These kingdoms flourished B.C. 1400 to 1000.

3.

"Saintly teachers, learned Brâhmans!
Welcome to my sacrifice!
Whoso of you be the wisest
Let him stand and win the prize!
Who is deepest in his lore,
Let him take the cows and gold,"
Thus unto the learned Brâhmans
Spoke Janaka, monarch bold!

4.

Brâhmans heard the royal mandate,
Durst not stand and claim the prize,
Where so many wise had gathered,
Who could claim to be most wise?
Up stood noble Yâjnavalkya,—
Janaka's great priest was he,—
Boldly spake unto his pupil,
"Drive the cattle home for me!"

5.

Wrathful were the other Brâhmans,—
Asvala, th' invoking priest,
Ârtabhâga, wise and saintly,
Lâhyâyani, great at feast,
Châkrâyana, Kaushîtaki,
Uddâlaka full of pride,
Many other wrathful sages
Yâjnavalkya's knowledge tried!

6.

Proudly stood great Yâjnavalkya,
Answered them with haughty pride,
As a great and towering mountain
Beateth back the surging tide!
Then stood Gârgî, saintly lady,
Noble hearted, fair and tall,
Learned as the wisest Brâhman,
Noblest in th' assembled hall!

7.

"As a warrior of the Kâsîs
Or Videha's warlike land
Lifts his bow with sound of thunder,
Lifts two arrows in his hand,
Even so, great Yâjnavalkya,
In this hall I challenge thee,
I will ask you but two questions,
Listen then and answer me.

8.

"On the earth, so far-extending,
In the firmament and sky,
In the present, past, and future,
Ever present, ever nigh,
Like the warp and like the woof
Woven in the space and sky,—
Wherein rests this universe,—
What is present, ever nigh?"

9.

To her answered Yâjnavalkya,
"Deep the question thou hast made!
It is ether, noble lady,
Which doth sky and earth pervade."
To him spake the noble lady,
"Good the answer you have given!
But this ether, Yâjnavalkya,
Wherein is it subtly woven?"

10.

"Listen, Gârgî, to my answer,
In th' IMMORTAL it is woven!
Of th' IMMORTAL who shall speak?
Listen, as in sâstras * given.
Not corporeal and not ether,
He is neither short nor long,
Flames not like the flaming red fire,
Nor like water flows along.

11.

"Without shadow, without darkness,
He is neither air nor sky,
Void of sensuous taste and feeling,
Dwells alone sublime and high!

* Holy works.

Without organs, without senses,
All the world He hears and sees,
Void of limbs, but ever active,
Void of form, but measureless!

12.

"Gârgî! wouldst then further fathom?
His great arm holds earth and sky!
Days and hours His mandates listen,
Sun and moon His hests obey!
He has shaped the snowy mountains,
Rolled the rivers swift and broad,
He directs all nature's actions,
He is Brahman, He is God!"

Abridged from the Brihadâranyaka Upanishad, III. 1, 8.

THE LEGEND OF MAITREYÎ.

I.

UNTO her,—his spouse beloved,—
  Maitreyî the pious-hearted,—
Thus spoke learned Yâjnavalkya,
  When to woods the saint departed.
"Maitreyî, my spouse beloved,
  All my wealth and goods I leave,
Take thy own, thy proper portion,
  Hers to Kâtyâyanî give!"

2

"Will thy wealth and worldly objects,"—
  Spake the pious-hearted wife,—
"Lead me to salvation holy,
  Lead me to immortal life?"
"Nay," said learned Yâjnavalkya,
  "Not unto immortal life,
But to life the rich man liveth
  Wealth will lead thee, gentle wife."

3.

"Vain to me the things that perish,
Lead not to immortal life,—
That which leads to true salvation,
Grant that wealth unto your wife!"
"Ever dear," said Yâjnavalkya,
"Dearer now thou art to me,
And the wealth which brings salvation,
I will grant that wealth to thee!

4.

"Saintly love of man and woman,
Love unto our brother men,
Love of parents, love of children,
Love unto our flocks and kine,
Love of every earthly object
Is but love of our own Soul,
Know thy Self, and love thy Self,
Thou knowest all, thou lovest all!

5.

"Sound the drum, a music issues,—
Canst thou grasp that music bold?
Blow the conch at festive season,
Its wild music canst thou hold?
Strike the deep and sounding lyre,
Canst thou grasp its voice profound?
But hold the drum, the conch, the lyre,
And you stop the uttered sound!

6.

"Love thy great and inner Self,
Know the one, the mighty Soul,
And thou lov'st the universe,
And in sooth thou knowest all!
From the fire a deep cloud issues,
Various-formed it floats on high,—
From the mighty Soul thus issues
Forms that people earth and sky!

7.

"He breathed forth the universe!
Vedas, Sâstras, all are His!
Senses and the inner souls,
Worlds, the mountains, and the seas!
Seest thou this transparent crystal?
Like this, without form is He!
He breathed forth this universe!
And the worlds will in Him be:"

8.

"My love! my lord!" Maitreyî said,
"Pardon, if I somewhat fail,—
Weak is woman's sense and reason,—
And obscure the truth you tell."
"Not so," Yâjnavalkya answered,
"Not obscure, but clear to all,—
Clear as is the sun of midday
Is that great immortal Soul!

9.

"Not from outer world distinct,—
  Pervading all, embracing all,—
Is that one directing force,
  Is that universal Soul!
Unseen, but ever manifest
  In the worlds and oceans broad,
Ever present, knowing all,
  He is Brahman! He is God!"

Abridged from Brihadâranyaka Upanishad, IV. 5.

THE LEGEND OF UMÂ.

I.

GODS and men and lower beings,—
  All from mighty Brahman flow!
But in vanity and blindness
  Brahman great, we do not know!
Once in past and ancient ages
  Vanity the gods o'ercame,—
Boastful of their power and glory,
  Knew not whence that prowess came!

2.

Brahman to the gods appeared,
  And they knew not who was He,—
Unto Agni thus they spake,—
  "Know thou who this stranger be."
Brahman placed a blade of straw,
  And the mighty god of Fire
Vainly strove to burn the blade,
  Went back in his shame and ire!

3.

Unto Vâyu, god of tempests,
Strong in might, resistless, free,
Spake the gods in secret terror,
"Know thou who this stranger be."
Brahman placed a blade of light straw,
On it mighty Vâyu came,
Vain he strove the blade to carry,
Went back in his ire and shame!

4.

Unto Indra, king of bright gods,
Highest in the realms or sky,
Spake the gods with soft entreaty,
"Know thou who this stranger be."
Indra unto Brahman came,
Knew not Brahman in his might,
Saw no stranger god before him,—
He had vanished from his sight!

5.

Radiant in her god-like splendour,
Umâ Haimavatî came!
Umâ of the northern mountains,—
Heavenly lore in mortal frame!
Of her Indra humbly questioned,
Who the stranger god might be,—
To him Umâ gently answered,
God of all the gods was He!

6.

" As the lightning's mighty splendour
  Fills the eye with dazzling light,
Knowledge of the mighty Brahman
  Fills the heart with radiance bright!
From Him flows, ye gods! your prowess,
  From Him worlds and oceans broad,
To Him lift your humble prayers,
  He is Brahman, He is God."

Abridged from Kena Upanishad, III., V.

THE LEGEND OF NACHIKETAS.

I.

NACHIKETAS, righteous boy,—
　By his father sent below,—
From the mighty king of Death,
　His great secret feign would know!
"There is doubt,"—so spake the boy—
　"When an earthly mortal dies,
Is that death his final end?—
　Or does he live in earth or skies?"

2.

Unto him thus answered Yama,
　"Nachiketas! you speak well,
Mortals often ask that question,
　Gods that question often feel!
Nachiketas! 'tis my secret,—
　Secret unto all unknown,—
Ask for every other favour,
　Death's great secret leave alone!

3.

"Ask for sons and happy grandsons—
They a hundred years will live,—
Ask for gold and cars and horses,—
Every blessing mortals crave!
Ask for broad and spacious acres,
Ask for harvests rich and rare,
Many autumns,—as thou willest,—
Live without a pang or fear!

4.

"Nachiketas! other objects
If thy anxious heart desire,
Ask for them,—for wealth or glory,—
Dread refusal nor my ire!
Be a king of mighty kingdoms,
Be a lord upon the earth,
Happy in thy life's fruition,
Be the foremost in thy worth!

5.

"Every wish thy heart can fathom,
Ask for joys on earth so rare;
With their cars and heavenly music
Take these heavenly damsels fair!
Be attended by these maidens,—
Such as they men do not see,—
Ask for these and other favours,
Leave my secret unto me!"

6.

"These are," Nachiketas answered,
"Objects that will fade away,
What will please us in the present,
Fade to-morrow and decay!
Keep thy dance and keep thy music,
For great objects let me pray,
Teach me thy great secret, Yama,—
Secret of the after-day!"

7.

Pressed by pious Nachiketas,
Death his secret thus revealed,
"To the man of contemplation
Life and Death their secret yield.
And he sees the ancient Soul,
Hid in dark from mortal eyes,
Sees the great and mighty Self,—
God pervading earth and skies!

8.

"And the man who knows this secret,
Comprehends and grasps it all,—
Casteth off his mortal body,
Mingles in the mighty Soul!
This, O mortal! is my secret,
Brahman is the mighty Breath!
Brahman's house is ever open,
Life existeth after death!"

Abridged from Katha Upanishad, I. 1, 2.

THE LEGEND OF BÂLÂKI.

1.

BÂLÂKI, a learned Brâhman,
Proud of knowledge, proud of lore,
Versed he was in many a sâstra,
Travelled many a distant shore.
In the land of Usînara,
And in Matsya he had been,
Panchâla and the Kuru kingdoms,
Videha and the Kâsî seen.*

2.

Ajâtasatru, learned monarch,
Ruled in Kâsî's mighty land,
Unto him repaired the Brâhman,
In his palace rich and grand.
"Blessed be thy rule, O monarch!
O'er this kingdom rich and broad,
I will speak to thee of Brahman,
I will speak to thee of God!"

* All these countries were in the Gangetic valley, and flourished about 1400 to 1000 B.C. The Usînara and the Matsya countries were to the west, lying along the Jumna river. Of the Kuru and the Panchâla kingdoms I have spoken before. The Videhas lived in North Behar, and the Kâsîs in the country round the site of modern Benares.

3.

" Welcome, welcome, learned priest ! "
    Ajâtasatru thus replied,—
" For thy holy speech accept
    A thousand kine of finest breed !
  Every learned Brâhman hies
    To Janaka, holy king,—
  Welcome thou to Kâsî's court,
    And a Brâhman's blessings bring ! "

4.

" List then, king ! to words of wisdom,"—
    Proud Bâlâki thus began,—
" Knowest thou the radiant Soul
    Dwelleth in the radiant sun ?
  Him I worship ! "—said Bâlâki.
    " Not so ! "—answered thus the king,
" For the sun is mighty glorious,
    But is a created thing ! "

5.

" Knowest thou the lunar crescent,
    Shining in the starry sky ?
  Knowest thou the beauteous Soul,
    Dwelleth there serene and high ?
  Him I worship ! "—said Bâlâki.
    " Not so ! "—answered thus the king,
" For the moon is bright and beauteous,
    But is a created thing ! "

6.

"Dost thou know the forked lightning,
Flashing through the lurid sky?
Dost thou know the dreaded Soul,
Dwelleth there, terrific, high?
Him I worship!"—said Bâlâki.
"Not so!"—answered thus the king,
"For the lightning is terrific,
But is a created thing!"

7.

"Dost thou know the deep-voiced thunder,
Pealing through the echoing sky?
Dost thou know the soul that dwelleth
In that sound, terrific, high?
Him I worship!"—said Bâlâki.
"Not so!"—answered thus the king,
"For the thunder is terrific,
But is a created thing!"

8.

Long he toiled, the learned Brâhman,
Power Almighty to explain,
Quoted he from holy sâstras,
Argued long, but argued vain!
To his reasons, to his learning,
Ever answered thus the king,
"Mighty wondrous is all nature,
But it is created thing!"

9.

Still he toiled, the learned Brâhman,
To explain the God on high,—
Spoke of fire and spoke of ether,
Spoke of water and of sky,
Spoke of shadow and reflection,
Spoke of echo and of sound,
Argued about dreams and slumber,
But solution none he found!

10.

Silently the boastful Brâhman
Bent his head in grief and shame,
Sad he was,—the learned Brâhman,—
To a wiser king he came!
"Thus far,"—said the monarch gently,
"Thus far doth thy wisdom go!"
"Thus far! wise and learned monarch!
Teach me what you further know!"

11.

With the fuel, meek and humble,
Bâlâki as student came,
Seeking knowledge from the monarch,*
Great in learning as in fame.

* "While the priestly caste was still multiplying rituals and supplying dogmatic explanations for each rite, the royal caste seems to have felt some impatience at this priestly pedantry. Thinking and earnest Kshatriyas asked themselves if these rites and dogmas were all that religion could teach. Learned Kshatriyas, while still conforming to

"He who made the sun and moon,
And the sky and earth so broad,
He who breathed all Nature forth,—
He is Brahman, He is God!"

Abridged from the Kaushîtaki Upanishad.

the rites laid down by priests, gave a start to healthier speculations, and inquired about the destination of the Soul and the nature of the Supreme Being. So bold, so healthy and vigorous were these new and earnest speculations, that the priestly classes, who were wise in their own esteem, at last felt their inferiority, and came to Kshatriyas to learn something of the wisdom of the new school."—*Civilisation in Ancient India*, vol. i. pp. 133, 134.

HYMN OF THE DYING MAN.

The following remarkable verses are to be uttered on the death-bed. They are the last three verses of the Upanishad from which they are translated.

I.

SOLE Rishi! Pushan! glorious Yama! *
  God of day! withdraw thy rays,
And let me once more view thy splendour,—
  View it with my closing eyes!
Let me once more view the light,
  The gladsome light that dwells in thee!
Th' Almighty Light which you reflect,—
  Th' Almighty Soul, it dwells in me!

2.

My breath will mingle with the air,
  To ashes turn this mortal frame,
Then turn, my soul, recall each deed,
  Each action done of praise or blame.
My hours of life are almost past,
  And steals o'er me the hand of death,
Then think, my soul, of actions done,
  Ere yet I yield this fleeting breath!

* All names of the sun.

3.

Agni! friend of dying mortals,*
  Lead me by the righteous path,
Let me win thy gracious blessings,
  Let me shun thy mighty wrath!
Lead me by the righteous path,
  In this last momentous hour,
Reverently I bend to Agni,
  In him—worship Brahman's power!

From the Îsâ Upanishad.

* Address to Fire,—in reference to the rite of cremation, which is considered beneficial to the departed.

III.

PASSAGES FROM BUDDHIST SCRIPTURES.

"The *Three Pitakas* were composed, settled, and arranged in India during the hundred or two hundred years after the death of Gautama (Buddha), just as the four Christian Gospels were composed and settled within a century or two after the death of Jesus. . . . The Three Pitakas are known as the Sutta Pitaka, the Vinaya Pitaka, and the Abhidhamma Pitaka. The works comprised in the Sutta Pitaka profess to record the sayings and doings of Gautama Buddha himself. . . . The Vinaya Pitaka contains very minute rules, often on the most trivial subjects, for the conduct of monks and nuns. . . . And lastly, the Abhidhamma Pitaka contains disquisitions on various subjects, on the conditions of life in different worlds, on personal qualities, on the elements, on the causes of existence, &c."

—*Civilisation in Ancient India*, vol. i. pp. 315, 316.

BUDDHA'S BIRTH.

1.

When was born our saintly Master,
Asita the Rishi found
Gods in all the sky assembled,
Wafting blessings, pleased in mind!
"Wherefore are they all assembled,
Wave their garments in the sky?
Wherefore," asked the mighty Rishi,
"Pleased in mind the gods on high?"
"'Tis because the saintly Master
For the good of all is born,
He is born among the Sâkyas,*
Fair Lumbini doth adorn!"

2.

Asita, the mighty Rishi,
Went unto the Sâkya king,
"Unto thee a babe is given,—
I to him my homage bring!"

* Kapilavastu, the capital town of the Sâkya clan, was situated on the banks of the Rohini river, to the north-east of modern Behar. Buddha was born about 557 B.C.

They brought the babe, like gold resplendent,
  Wrought and shaped by skilful hand,
Beaming with an inward glory,
  Jewel of the blessed land!
"He is the auspicious Master,"
  So the sage Asita said,
"He will be the great *awakened*,
  Rule of righteousness will spread."

3.

And the blind received their sight,
  Longing for the babe to see!
And the deaf they heard again,
  Heard his words of piety!
And the dumb they spoke again
  Of the saintly Master come!
And the crooked men were straight,
  Walked forth free the halt and lame!
Chains and shackles broke and fell
  In the prisons of the earth!
And the blue and joyous sky
  Hailed the saintly Master's birth!

From the Nâlaka Sutta and Birth Stories.

BUDDHA'S DEATH.

1.

THUS in many lands they wandered,
  Buddha and his faithful friend,
Teaching truth to many nations,
  Till his life approached its end.
And they say, along the pathway,
  As the saintly Master went,
Fruit trees blossomed out of season
  And a lovely fragrance lent!
And that flowers and sandal-powder
  Gently fell on him from high,
And came strains of heavenly music
  Gently wafted from the sky!

2.

But the saintly Master whispered
  To his friend beloved and blest,
"'Tis not thus, O friend Ânanda!
  That the Buddha's honoured best.
Not by flowers or sandal-powder,
  Not by music's heavenly strain,
Is the soul's true worship rendered,
  Useless are these things and vain!

But the brother and the sister,
Man devout and woman holy,—
Pure in life, in duty faithful,—
They perform the worship truly!"

3.

Night came on, and saintly Buddha
Slept in suffering, sick and wan,
When a Brâhman, seeking wisdom,
Came to see the holy man.
Anxiously Ânanda stopped him,
But spoke Buddha, though in pain,
"He who comes to seek for wisdom
Shall not come to me in vain!"
And he to the pious stranger
Told the truth in language plain,
Taught the law with dying accents,
Stopped, and never spoke again!

From the Mahâparinirvana Sutta.

TEN PRECEPTS FROM DHAMMAPADA.

"The whole of the *Dhammapada* is a string of 423 moral precepts which for their beauty and moral worth are unsurpassed by any similar collection of precepts made in any age or country. . . . Who is not struck by the remarkable coincidence of these noble precepts with those preached five hundred years after in Palestine by the gentle and pure-souled Jesus Christ?"—*Civilisation in Ancient India*, vol. i. p. 366, 367.

Return Love for Hatred.

HATE for hatred if ye render,
  Hatred lives and mortal strife;
Love return for bitter hatred,
  Hatred dies, and sweet is life! (5)

Precepts without Acts.

Pious precepts, gentle friend,
  Never acted, wisely meant,
Are like gay and coloured flowers,—
  Without fragrance, without scent! (51)

The Golden Rule.

As you dread all pain and suffering,
  Love your life and death abhor,
So doth every living creature,
  Harm not things that live and breathe.
(129, 130)

Live without Hatred among Men you Hate.

With the men who live in hatred
  Ye shall live devoid of hate,
Unto men who smite in anger
  Show your love and meekness great. (197)

Good Works survive.

Good works done endure for ever,
  And in higher life will meet,
E'en as gentle loving kinsmen
  Home-returning kinsmen greet! (200)

Overcome Anger by Love.

Anger by your love o'ermaster,
  Good for evil acts return;
By charity the miser conquer,
  By your truth let false men learn! (223)

The Faults of other Men.

Faults of other men ye question,
  Not the fault that ye have done!
Like chaff your neighbour's vices winnow,
  Like a false die hide your own! (252)

The Elder and the Sage.

Not an Elder, not a Sage,
Is the man advanced in age;
Truth and virtue, love and pureness,
Make the Elder and the Sage. (260, 261)

Assumed and True Holiness.

Not by skins and plaited hair.
Not by family or birth,
But by truth and righteousness
Is the Brâhman known on earth. (393)

There is Ravening within.

Wherefore wear the plaited hair,
Wherefore garment wild of skin,
What avails this outward penance
When there's raveuing within! (394)

IV.

EDICTS OF ASOKA.

"If a man's fame can be measured by the number of hearts who revere his memory, by the number of lips who have mentioned and still mention him with honour, Asoka is more famous than Charlemagne or Cæsar."

—*Kopen, quoted in Rhys Davids' Buddhism*, p. 222.

He ruled over Northern India from about 260 to 222 B.C., embraced the Buddhist religion, and spread it over India, as Constantine the Great spread Christianity over the Roman Empire five centuries later.

MESSAGE TO HIS PEOPLE.

1.

THUS speaks royal Piyadasi,*
  Of the gods beloved,
To his many subject nations,
  Peoples he has loved:—
I have carved on rocks and pillars
  Rules my men obey,
And my Dharma-mahâmâtras †
  Point to them the way.

2.

Royal highways in my empire
  Are by mangoes shaded,
Wells and inns refresh and cheer
  The thirsty and the jaded.
But a mission greater, holier,—
  To refresh the soul!
To relieve the thirsty heart,
  And comfort bring to all!

* The name assumed by Asoka in all his inscriptions.

† Officers employed to teach religion and moral precepts to the people.

3.

Amongst my men of every sect,
Amongst the Brâhmans holy,
Amongst all sects of mendicants,
Amongst Nirgranthas * lowly,
My Mahâmâtras ever work
For holy righteousness,
They work to show the pious way,
To show the path of peace !

4.

Would'st thou know that pious way,
That righteous path of peace,—
It is the way that leads to joy,
To joy and holy bliss !
Religion !—'tis another name
For Truth and Charity,
Religious rite and sacrifice
Is Kindness, Purity !

5.

Some would spread Religious faith
By strong compulsive laws,—
Gentle lessons and persuasion,
Be still Asoka's ways !

* The learned Brâhmans were generally orthodox Hindus who kept aloof from Buddhism, the religion of the people. The Nirgranthas were a sect of Jainas who went about unclad, and renounced all worldly things.

I value inward inspiration,—
  Awakening of the heart,—
Not a formal blind compliance
  With rules that we impart.

6.

With this view this righteous edict
  This year * I promulgate,
May it teach my sons and grandsons
  And my people great!
May it unto after ages
  Like sun and moon endure,
May it in this life, and after,
  Righteous bliss secure!

From Pillar Edict, VIII

* The year is mentioned in the text, being twenty-seven years after Asoka's coronation. The date of the edict is therefore about 233 B.C.

MESSAGE TO FOREIGN NATIONS.

1.

FAR, far extend Kalinga's plains,
 And Bengal's fertile coast;
Asoka, of the gods beloved,
 There sent his conquering host.
They slaved a hundred thousand men,
 A hundred thousand died,—
"And is this what a conquest means?"
 The pious monarch cried!

2.

"Brâhmans pure and Srâmans good,
 And men who toil in life;
Parents to their children dear,
 Fond husband, weeping wife,—
These I've killed, enslaved and sold,
 And bade the helpless die!"
A throb was on the monarch's brow,
 A tear was in his eye!

3.

Repentance wrung his royal breast,
 And he was meek and lowly ;
And virtuous wishes filled his soul,
 And aspirations holy.
He thought of Sâkya, noble Teacher,
 Buddha, high of birth,
Who left his throne and toiled for men,
 And spread good will on earth !

4.

" Ho ! other conquests I will spread,
 And other trophies win,"—
The pious monarch thus he cried,—
 " I'll conquer crime and sin !
Unto the frontiers of my realm,
 And far beyond, proclaim,
Asoka fights in faith alone,
 And wins the righteous fame !

5.

" To Antiochus, Syria's lord,
 To Egypt's Ptolemy,
To Antigonus, mighty king
 Of Macedon the free,

To Magas of Cyrene fair,
　To Alexander, king
Of mountain-covered Epiros,*—
　The joyful tidings bring!

6.

"To far Kâverî's fertile banks,
　Where mighty Cholas live,
To Kumârikâ's distant point,
　Where Pândya clans still thrive,
To Tâmraparni's verdant isle,
　For pearls well known to fame,
To Henarâja Vismâvasi †
　The joyful news proclaim!

7.

"To our friends the Bactrian Greeks,
　And to the bold Kambojas,
To Nâbhakas and Nâbhapantis,
　And to the sturdy Bhojas,

* These kings of Syria, Egypt, Macedon, Cyrene, and Epiros were contemporaries of Asoka; and Asoka sent missionaries to proclaim Buddhism in their countries. The Essenes of Syria and the Therapeuts of Egypt were the results of these missions.

† The Cholas, Cheras, and Pândyas were the greatest powers in India south of the Krishnâ river in the olden times. Kumârikâ is Cape Comorin, and Tâmraparni is Ceylon. Henarâja Vismâvasi was in Southern India.

To Petenikas in the south,
To Andhras in Deccan,
To far Pulindas tell the news,*—
Tell it to every man!"

8.

Far and wide the news they told,
And Buddha's faith proclaimed;
Strange nations Buddha's precepts learnt,†
His holy name they named.
Asoka felt a joy intense,
His life's great work was done,
For he had won the righteous fame,
And fought in faith alone!

From Rock Edict, XIII.

* This and the previous paragraph throw light on the geography of India in the third century B.C. The Bactrian Greeks and the Kambojas of Kabul lived on the western frontier. The Nâbhakas and Nâbhapantis lived in Central India, and the Bhojas in Malwa. The Petenikas had their capital, Pratisthâna, on the Godâvari river. The Andhras were the mightiest race in the Deccan, and the Pulindas also lived in Southern India.

† Over two centuries before the birth of Christ, Buddhist missionaries preached in Syria those noble moral precepts which we find in the Christian gospels. The Essenes, a sect of western Buddhists, were still thriving and preaching these precepts when Jesus was born.

V.

KÂVYA POETRY.

"The three centuries (500 to 800 A.D.) commencing with the time of Vikramâditya the Great may be called the Augustan era of Sanscrit literature, and nearly all the great works which are popular in India to this day belong to this period. *Kâlidâsa* wrote his matchless dramas and poems in Vikrama's court. *Amara Sinha*, the lexicographer, was another of the "nine gems" of this court. And Bhâravi was Kâlidâsa's contemporary, or lived shortly after. *Sîlâditya II.*, a successor of Vikramâditya, ruled from 610 to 650 A.D., and is the reputed author of Ratnâvali. *Daudin*, the author of Dasakumâra Charita, was an old man when Sîlâditya II. reigned, and *Bânabhatta*, the author of Kâdamvarî, lived in his court. *Subandhu*, the author of Vâsavadattâ, also lived at the same time; and there are reasons to believe that the Bhattikavya was composed by *Bhartrihari*, the author of the Satakas, in the same reign.

"In the next century Yasovarman ruled between 700 and 750 A.D., and the renowned *Bhavabhûti* composed his powerful dramas in this reign. Bhavabhûti, however, was the last of the galaxy of poets and literary men of Ancient India, and no great literary genius arose in India after the eighth century.

"It was in this Augustan era also that the great national Epics of India, the production of many ages, received their last additions and touches, and assumed their final shape; and the voluminous Purânas, which have given their name to this period, began to be composed in their present shape.

"In modern Hindu science, too, we have the brightest names in these three centuries. Âryabhatta, the founder of modern Hindu astronomy, was born in 476 A.D., and produced his work early in the sixth century. Varâhamihira, his successor, was one of the "nine gems" of Vikrama's court. And Brahmagupta was born in 598 A.D."

—*Civilisation in Ancient India*, vol. i. pp. 18, 19.

THE PENANCE OF UMÂ.

Umâ, in the extract given before from the Kena Upanishad, is divine intelligence, explaining to the celestial powers the nature of Brahman or God. In later times, however, she acquired a more distinct personality, and was considered to be the daughter of the god of the Himâlayas, and the consort of Siva or Sambhu, one of the Hindu Trinity. Her marriage with Siva is the subject of the beautiful poem of Kâlidâsa from which the following portion has been translated.

1.

Long through sultry Summer evenings
  Did her mighty penance last,
Long through Rains and through the Autumn,
  In the Dews and Winter's blast.

2.

And when Spring the green woods mantled *
  With its verdure soft and green,
To the hermitage a Brâhman
  Came, attired in barks and skin.

3.

And in language sweet and courteous
  Questioned Umâ of her rite,
Asked her of her plants and creepers,
  Asked her of the rills so bright.

* The Hindus reckon six seasons in the year, viz., Spring, Summer, Rains, Autumn, Dews, and Winter, each season lasting two months.

4.

"Not by Gangâ's holy waters
Are these sacred mountains graced,
Umâ! as by righteous actions,
By thy holy penance blest!

5.

"But a doubt in me ariseth,
Pardon if too far I go,—
Brâhmans are by nature curious,
Seek for hidden thoughts to know.

6.

"Thou art born of noble parents,
Decked with world-surpassing beauty!
In thy youth and in thy splendour
Why this penance,—this sad duty?

7.

"Noble ladies, stung with sorrow,
Oft engage in pious rite,—
In thy father's happy mansions,
Can grief touch thee, maiden bright?

8.

"Wherefore leaves and barks of wild trees
Dim thy blooming beauty bright?
Does the morning's paler glamour
Suit the moonlit starry night?

9.

"Not for joys of heaven this penance,
For this realm is like the sky;
And for worthy noble suitor
Need a beauteous maiden sigh?

10.

"Yet that sigh, that heaving bosom
Tells of disappointed love!
To a maiden of thy beauty
Can a suitor cruel prove?

11.

"Can he heartless view that beauty
By the red sun tinged and shaded?
Can he view thy toil-worn visage
Like moon's crescent pale and faded?

12.

"But, perchance, my gentle Umâ,
Of some service I may be,
I have done some holy penance,
Thine its fruit and blessings be!"

13.

Silent Umâ dropped a tear-drop,
Told her maid the tale to tell,
And the maid unto the Brâhman
Told the sad and piteous tale.

14.

"List, O youth! The pious maiden,
Spurning all the gods of sky,
Lifts her heart, with love so tender,
To great Sambhu, lord on high!

15.

"In her father's glorious mansions
Found the maid no peace, no rest,
In the cool and snow-decked grottoes
Ever burnt with love her breast!

16.

"Oft in midnight's lonely silence
Weeping, she of Sambhu sung,
Till the nymphs of woods and mountains
Wept to hear her plaintive song!

17.

"And when came the dreary morning,
Starting from a loving dream,
Umâ clasped the empty shadow,
Called for Sambhu in a scream!

18.

"Brooding on her luckless passion,
She has left her father's home,
To engage in mighty penance,
In this wilderness to roam!"

19.

Smiling answered then the Brâhman,
"Is it true, my lovely maid,
All this penance pure and holy
That unlovely god to wed?

20.

"Will thy hand so soft and tender
Clasp his hands where snakes entwine?
Will thy rich and bridal garment
On his red skins beauteous shine?

21.

"Wilt thou with such bridegroom wander
Over funeral sites unblest?
With the impure funeral ashes
Wilt thou stain thy gentle breast?

22.

"Obscure his birth! Unknown his wealth!
Unworthy he of thy bright grace!
On holy sites, not funeral places,
Pious men their altars raise!"

23.

Angry Umâ heard the Brâhman
Speaking thus of Sambhu high;
Her red lips quivered in her anger,
Shone her dark and flashing eye!

24.

"Little knowest of great Sambhu,"
  Thus the angry maid replied ;
"Lofty souls of unknown splendour
  Flippant mortals will deride !

25.

"Mighty Refuge of Creation !—
  Will he seek for paltry gain ?
Arbiter of other's fortunes !—
  Doth he reck what is his own ?

26.

"Wandering in dark funeral places,—
  Yet of worlds the Lord is he !
Wearing shape, sublime, terrific,—
  Yet he showers his blessings free !

27.

"Unknown his birth ! For mighty Brahmâ
  Does he know of Sambhu's birth ?
Unknown his power ! For gods celestial,
  Do they know of Sambhu's worth ?

28.

"But cease these words,—and, learned Brâhman !
  Leave me, and in peace depart !
If small his virtues, great his failings,—
  Sambhu still doth fill this heart !"

29.

Uprose the maiden in her anger,
  Rose and quickly turned away;
But the Brâhman held her garment,
  Boldly stopped the maiden's way.

30.

She turned to chide,—it was her Sambhu,—
  Now in glorious form divine!
"Won by love and won by penance,
  Gentle Umâ! I am thine!"

Abridged from Kâlidâsa's Kumâra-sambhava, V.

THE CONQUESTS OF RAGHU.

The piece translated below is important, as it throws light on the geography of India at the time of the poet, *i.e.*, in the sixth century after Christ.

I.

EASTWARD marched Ayodhyâ's monarch,
Conquering many a sturdy foe,
Till he reached the mighty ocean,
On whose shores the palm trees grow.

2.

Suhma's * monarch saved his kingdom,
Bowing to the conqueror brave,—
Supple cane-twigs bend as meekly
'Neath the strong resistless wave.

3.

Bengal's kings came with their war-boats,
Bravely fought, but fought in vain;
And the victor built a pillar
Where great Gangâ meets the main.

* Supposed to be an ancient kingdom in East Bengal.

4.

Rice transplanted yields a harvest!
So unto the victor brave,
Conquered kings to thrones restoréd
Presents and rich offerings gave.

5.

Tuskers formed a bridge most wondrous
O'er the broad Kapisâ's stream; *
Utkal's monarch † led the victor
To Kalinga's mighty realm. ‡

6.

Fiercely fought Kalinga's monarch
On his tusker great in height;
But in vain his arrows showered
On the victor, proud in might!

7.

And on beds of spreading betel
Soldiers sat and drank the wine;
And Kalinga's fame and glory
With the wine they seemed to drain!

* The Suvarnarekhâ river.

† Northern Orissa.

‡ The great Kalinga kingdom stretched from Orissa to the Krishnâ river in the south.

8.

But the great and noble victor
Placed the king again on throne,
Gave him back his wealth and empire,
Robbed him of his fame alone!

9.

Southward marched Ayodhyâ's monarch
By the azure sparkling sea,
And through forests of the nut-palm
Marched his soldiers bold and free!

10.

Crossed Kâverî, mighty river,
Stopped where steep Malayas rise;
Steeds they tied in spicy forests,
Tuskers to the sandal trees.

11.

Mighty Pândyas,* brave in combat,
Vainly with great Raghu fought;
And with pearls from Ceylon's island
Mighty Raghu's grace they sought.

* One of the three great nations who lived in the extreme south of India. We have found their name mentioned in the edicts of Asoka.

12.

Across the lofty Sahya mountains *
Mighty Raghu forced his way,
Far Kerala's † soft-eyed maidens
Saw his troops and fled away.

13.

Northwards now Ayodhyâ's monarch
Went the Persian chiefs ‡ to quell;
Pale-faced Yavan § women wept
For the chiefs who fought and fell.

14.

Fiercely fought each western warrior
On his fiery warlike horse;
But the victor's swords and arrows
Swept and thinned the hostile force.

* The Western Ghats.

† The Kerala kingdom lay to the west of the Western Ghats, corresponding to modern Travancore.

‡ The Shah kings of Gujrat ruled till about 400 A.D. In the fifth century the Gupta kings of Kanouj were on friendly terms with the kings of Persia. In the sixth century the great Nausharwan ruled in Persia.

§ The Yavanas or Bactrian Greeks were independent till about 130 B.C. They then settled in various parts of Western India.

15.

Now the victor's warlike soldiers
  Rested in the fields of vine,*
Spread the deer-skin on the heather,
  Gaily quaffed the fresh grape-wine.

16.

Northwards then great Raghu travelled,
  And his tuskers crossed the sands;
Scented pollen on them showered,
  Wafted from the northern lands.

17.

Fiery Huns are fierce and warlike,†—
  Vainly fought with Kosal's chief!
Women with their ruddy faces
  Wept for warriors in their grief.

18.

Kamboja's great and sturdy warriors ‡
  Quailed before Ayodhyâ's king;
Gold and fiery steeds of battle
  They unto the victor bring.

* Apparently Kabul, the land of grapes.

† The Huns invaded India in the fifth century after Christ, and had a kingdom in the Punjab in the sixth century. Their ruddy complexion is alluded to by the poet.

‡ A Kabul tribe.

19.

Then the hosts of mighty Raghu
Climbed the heights of Himalay,
Beating back the stubborn hill-tribes,
Eastwards now they forced their way.

20.

And they crossed great Ganga's waters,
Crossed Lohityâ's * sea-like wave;
And the lord of Pragjyotisha †
Quaked before the victor brave.

21.

With the tuskers of his country
Kamrup's lord had met his foes,—
Now those tuskers came as presents
To where Raghu's tents arose.

22.

Thus great Raghu, king of monarchs,
Conquering nations far and wide,
Back returned to fair Ayodhyâ,
Ruled with glory and with pride.

Abridged from Kâlidâsa's Raghu-vansa, IV.

* The Brahmaputra. † Assam.

MUKTÂLATÂ, PRINCESS OF CEYLON.

Kshemendra is a voluminous but not a great poet, and flourished in Kashmir in the eleventh century after Christ. His versification is fluent and graceful, and he seems to have condensed all that was best in older Sanscrit literature—poetry, rhetoric, tales, and fiction—into compact readable works. Buddhist stories too did not come amiss to him, and in his *Kalpalatâ* he gives us 108 Buddhist tales, one of which is given below. This work, *Kalpalatâ*, like most other Buddhist works, was lost in India, but my respected friend, Mr. Sarat Chandra Das, has during his journeys in Thibet recovered a copy of the work with a Thibetan translation, which is being published now by the Asiatic Society of Bengal.

1.

LIKE the bright moon's golden crescent,
Rising from the milky sea,
She was born with heavenly beauty
In Siṃhala * bright and free.

2.

On her birth a shower of bright pearls
From the skies auspicious fell;
Hence they named her Muktâlatâ,†
Princess of Siṃhala's isle.

* Ceylon.

† Which means a Pearl Creeper.

3.

And she grew in grace and brightness,
Lankâ's royal house to bless;
And as worth brings sweet contentment,
So her years brought loveliness.

4.

Merchants from the famed Srâvasti,
Happily it so befell,
Crossed the vast and perilous ocean,
Came to trade in Lankâ's isle.

5.

And they sung the sacred *Gâthâs*,
As their nightly sleep they sought;
Sung the holy lay which teaches
Precepts that our Master taught.

6.

From her inner palace chambers
Muktâ heard the beauteous song;
Bade the merchants to her presence,
Asked them what it was they sung.

7.

And they told the raptured maiden,
"Princess! it is Buddha's word!
He is bounteous to all creatures,
Of all creatures he is Lord!"

8.

And the gentle-hearted princess
  Raptured heard great Buddha's name;
And a brightness flushed her forehead,
  And a tremor shook her frame!

9.

Eagerly the pea-fowl listens
  To the cloud, presaging rain:
Eagerly the princess listened,
  Who this Lord?—she asked again.

10.

To the princess, pious-hearted,
  By her questions gratified,
Spoke the merchants of great Buddha,
  Lord of all creation wide.

11.

By the merchants' tale reminded
  Of her previous humble birth,
Unto them she gave a letter
  For great Buddha, Lord of earth.

12.

And the traders crossed the ocean,
  Reached their own, their native land,
Spoke to Buddha of the princess,
  Gave her letter in his hand.

13.

And our Master, all fore-knowing,—
  Knowing all by power of thought,—
Moved by tenderness and mercy,
  Thus perused the maiden's note!

14.

"Thy remembrance merit bringeth,
  Cures the longings of this world,
And imparting righteous knowledge
  Is like nectar to me, Lord!"

15.

Thus our Master, blessed Buddha,
  Briefly read the loving note,
And a gentle smile betokened
  All the workings of his thought.

16.

And with skill and knowledge wondrous,
  Which the painters never knew,
For the princess of Siṃhala
  On a sheet his likeness drew.

17.

By his mandate all the merchants
  In their vessels sailed anew,
Reached Siṃhala,—to the princess
  Gave the sheet our Master drew.

18.

And the people viewed the painting
Placed upon a golden shelf,
And with honour contemplating
Seemed t' attain the Lord himself!

19.

Written under that sweet likeness,
All the people, wondering truly,
Saw the holy Three Asylums,
Saw the Five Instructions holy!

20.

And the Noble Eightfold Path,
Sweetly writ, with wisdom rife,
With the Doctrine of Causation,—
Life to death, and death to life!

21.

Blazing bright in golden letters,
On it shone the Holy Word,—
Truth explained in beauteous language,
Written by our blessed Lord.

22.

"Sufferers from life's bitter sorrows!
Issue from your mansions drear,
Worldly objects snake-like strangle!
Trust in Buddha, cast all fear."

23.

And the monarch's noble daughter
Viewed the likeness fair and holy,
And was freed from all the longings
Bred of ignorance and folly.

24.

Tall and fair his golden likeness,
Broad his shoulders, mighty arms,
Eyes in contemplation closéd,
Stately nose and manly charms!

25.

Beauteous all in nature's beauty,
Ears and locks by art unaided,
Clad in russet bark,—like mountain
By the evening's red cloud shaded!

26.

Teaching duty by his bearing,
By his bright face teaching good,
Mercy and forbearance teaching,—
Such the form the princess viewed!

27.

Bowing, till the budding blossoms
From her ears and ringlets rained,
With them earthly joys discarding,
ruth supreme the princess gained.

28.

In a moment's time achieving
  Truth divine and knowledge rare,
Lost in joy and pious wonder
  Thus in gladness spoke the fair.

29.

"Chaser of the world's illusions,
  Saintly Buddha, dwelling far,
Present by this radiant likeness,
  Lovelier than the lotus fair!

30.

"I have crossed the world's illusions,
  Heart's true concentration found,
Passions, troubles are discarded,
  Peace, like nectar, flows around!"

31.

Thus she spoke, and unto Buddha
  Pearls and costly jewels sent;
For the use of holy *Sangha*
  With these gifts the merchants went.

32.

O'er the sea, unto our Master,
  In their ships the merchants came,
Bowing unto him they rendered
  Pearls and many a costly gem.

33.

And our Master kindly listened
To the tale the merchants told.
Questioned by the monk Ânanda
Unto him he thus revealed.

34.

"Rohiká, a servant maiden,
In a Sâkya's house who stayed,
She is born as Muktâlatâ,
By her worth a princess made!

35.

"Mahâdhana, princely merchant,
In Benares lived of yore,
And his wife, a virtuous woman,
Ratnâvatî name she bore.

36.

"And when died this Mahâdhana,
Ratnâvatî, childless fair,
On a lofty holy *stûpa*
Placed a necklace rich and rare.

37.

"For this action, elevated,
She as Muktâlatâ shone,
Born as Lankâ's beauteous princess
Now she has *Nirvâna* won!

38.

"She it was, whom pride of treasures
Maddened in a previous birth,
Hence, a while, as servant maiden
She was born and served on earth!

39.

"Deeds that are by mortals rendered,
Good or bad on this our earth,
Yield their fruits in equal measure
Ripened in a future birth!

40.

"Virtue is a beauteous creeper,
Rooted well in noble worth,
Bearing fame as scented blossoms,
Bearing fruits most sweet on earth!

41.

"Evil life is poisonous creeper,
Rooted in dark deeds of blame,
Yielding dire delusions only,
Endless misery and shame!

42.

"In this life's wild dreary desert,
Shun, ye men, all deeds of sin;
Bitter are the woes that follow,
Sorrows and repentance keen!

43.

"In the acts of grace rejoicing,
  Ever deeds of virtue do,
Moistened by the dew of Mercy
  Sweet the fruits of Virtue grow!"

From Kshemendra's Kalpalatá, VII.

VI.

THE HUNTER AND THE HERO.

The poem is known as *Kirâtârjunîyam* in Sanscrit, and was composed by Bhâravi, who lived in the sixth century after Christ. It is based on the story of the great epic Mahâbhârata. Yudhishthira, the eldest of the five Pândava brothers, the heroes of the epic, has lost his kingdom at a game of dice, and has retired with his brothers and wife to the forest. He sends a forester as a spy to observe how his rival Duryodhana is ruling the kingdom. The spy returns to the exiled king, and the poem begins with his account of Duryodhana's conduct and administration.

What follows is narrated in the poem itself. Yudhishthira's wife and brother Bhîma counsel instant war, but Yudhishthira inclines to moderation, and nobly adheres to his plighted word by which he relinquished his kingdom. The great saint Vyâsa then appears on the scene, and advises Arjuna, the third of the Pândava brothers, to win celestial arms by penance. Arjuna follows the advice, and engages himself in penances in the Himâlayas.

Indra, the chief of the minor gods, has attained his high position by penance, and is jealous of mortals who adopt the same means for attaining the same end. He sends down heavenly nymphs to disturb Arjuna's penances, and then himself descends in the shape of an anchorite to dissuade Arjuna from the rites in which he is engaged. But Arjuna is proof against temptation and against persuasion. The poet's descriptions of the peaceful penances which Arjuna performs accoutred in arms, of the winning but vain blandishments of the nymphs, of Indra's solicitation and advice, and of Arjuna's lofty determination and devotion to his purpose, are among the finest and most spirited passages in Sanscrit literature.

Indra fails to dissuade Arjuna from his rites, and at last reveals himself, and advises Arjuna to worship Siva, one of the Hindu Trinity, for the coveted celestial arms. Arjuna therefore engages once more in penances, and at last Siva appears before him in the guise of a wild hunter. He picks a quarrel with the mortal, and engages in a combat with him. Pleased with Arjuna's might and heroism, Siva bestows on him the celestial arms, and the poem closes with a hymn to Siva, unsurpassed in its piety and pathos.

The original poem is in eighteen Books, and I have been constrained to abridge it in two places. The description of the nymphs and their blandishments extends to four Books in the original, and I have compressed it into one in the translation, for even celestial charms might cloy if described in the fulness of the original! And the combat between Siva and Arjuna and its happy sequel, which have been described in six Books in the original, have been compressed into two Books in the translation. Feats of arms have ever been recognised as a fit subject of romance and song, but the shade of the poet must pardon his translator if he hesitates to follow him in those prolonged flights of poetry in which the poet is sustained only by the sonorous beauty of his language and the incomparable vigour of his expression. The Appendix given at the close of the translation will point out to the student of Sanscrit which verses of Books VII. to X. in the original have been rendered in Book VII. of the translation, and which verses of the poet's Books XIII. to XVIII. have been rendered in my Books X. to XII. The remaining Books of the original have been translated in full, verse for verse.

BOOK I.

DRAUPADÍ'S REMONSTRANCE.

SENT in hermit's guise to spy
  How Kuru's monarch ruled his men,
A forester, his task performed,
  Yudhishthir met in Dvaita's glen.
He bowed and spoke, nor pained his bosom
  Of the foeman's rule to tell,
Nor seek those men with accents false
  To please our ear who wish us well.
On vengeful thoughts intent, the monarch
  Bade the spy his tale unfold;
And sweet in language, rich in import,
  Clear in sense, the words he told. (3)

"Great monarchs see but through their spies,
  And spies should ne'er deceive their lord;
Forgive my speech if plain or pleasing,
  Seldom true is honied word!
False friend! who teaches not his king,
  False king! who hears not what they tell;
Where king and friends in truth agree,
  Fortune's favours love to dwell!

We foresters are simple men,
  And hard a king's designs to trace;
And if thy foeman's plans I ken,
  'Tis by thy kindness, by thy grace! (6)

"Seated on his throne he trembles
  At thee,—dwelling in the wood!
The realm he won by trick of dice
  He rules by righteous laws and good.
Deep in wiles, he would surpass thee
  In his fame for righteousness;
Better far to war with true men
  Than to consort with the base!
His passions veiled, by Manu's laws
  He seeks the virtuous path to tread;
By night and day his task dividing,
  Seeks a righteous fame to spread.
He treats his menials as his friends,
  And as his kinsmen friends withal;
Veiling his wrath he seeks to prove
  How conquering love rules over all!
With love impartial, equal care,
  He cultivates all virtues well;
And by his worth all varied virtues
  In harmonious concert dwell!
His kindness never lacks in gifts,
  His gifts with courteous manners flow,
And his courtesy and his favours
  Only men of virtue know.
Not for wealth and not in anger,
  Ever seeking righteous cause,

On his foe or on his children
  Visits sins with equal laws.
Placing trusty guards around him,
  Ever wears a fearless mien;
And wealth bestowed at sacrifices
  Speaks his gratitude to men.
And by careful thought devised,
  His plans, with steady toil pursued,
Open out a prosperous future,
  And conjointly lead to good! (15)

"Cars and horses of great chieftains
  Throng his palace court around;
Tuskers sent by mighty monarchs
  With their perfume * moist the ground.
And Kuru's lands are rich in harvests
  Ripening without tiller's toil;
Ask no rain, since Kuru's monarch
  Showers his blessings on the soil.
His bounteous and his peaceful rule
  To plenty and to wealth give birth;
Attracted by his godlike worth
  Spontaneous yields her wealth the earth.
Mighty chiefs, by wealth attracted,
  Warriors famed in many a strife,
Against their monarch never muster,
  Serve his cause even with their life.
His task performed, by trusty spies
  He learns the plans of other kings;

* Elephants are supposed at certain seasons to exude a perfumed juice from their temples.

His secret plan is only known,
  Like Heaven's designs, by fruits it brings!
His bow is never strung nor raised,
  Nor doth a frown his face o'erspread;
His kindly rule the chieftains cherish
  Like a garland on their head!
Strong in his rule, he now hath placed
  Duhsasan * young in kingly power:
With offerings due, in holy rites,
  By Indra told, he worships Fire!
His foes are quelled, his future glorious,
  And his realm extends to sea;
But strife with great men ends in sorrow,—
  And Duryodhan quakes at thee!
If thy name is spoke in converse,
  Quakes at Arjun's might of arm,
Bends in grief his anguished forehead,
  Like a snake by *Mantra's* charm!
Prepared he is to do thee battle;
  Take then, lord, precautions meet;
We gather words by others spoken,—
  Such, I lay them at thy feet." (25)

This said, the woodman went away,
  By Yudhishthir honoured well;
And the king in Bhîma's presence
  To Draupadî told the tale.†

* Duryodhana's younger brother.

† Bhima was the second brother, and Draupadî the wife of Yudhishthira.

She heard the tale of foemen's glory,
Thought of wrongs which they had done,
And to rouse her husband's anger
Drupad's daughter thus began. (27)

"Counsel to a saintly monarch
Is rebuke from woman weak;
But ignoring woman's duty,
Pardon if my feelings speak!
Of thy race the godlike monarchs
Held their rule o'er all this land;
But as tuskers hurl their garlands,
Thou hast hurled it from thy hand!
Weak are they who with the wily
Deal not with responding wile;
For like shafts on mail-less warriors,
Artful foemen on them steal!
Glory, in thy race begotten,
Won by valour, dear as wife,
Who but thee such glory forfeits,
Girt by warriors tried in strife? (31)

"Godlike man! now sadly treading
Paths despised by proud and free,
Doth not raging wrath consume thee
Even as flames the sapless tree?
Men spontaneous yield to heroes
Who in might subdue all ills,
For an all-forgiving creature
Love nor friend nor foeman feels!

Sandal decked great Bhîma's person !
  Dusty, now, he roams the hills !
Scarce I know, O soul of virtue !
  If my lord compassion feels !
Arjun, conquering northern nations,
  To the poor all treasures gave !
God-like Arjun, clad in wild barks,
  Doth he thy compassion move ?
Does my lord in patience witness
  Yonder twins,* so great, so good ?—
Dwelling uncouth in this forest
  Even like tuskers of the wood !
Scarce I guess thy feelings, monarch,
  Strange and various are our hearts,
But the thought of thy great sorrow
  Cruel grief to me imparts.
Erst you slept on couches sumptuous,
  Waked to hear the song of praise ;
Now on thorny earth reclining,
  Hear the sound the jackals raise !
Erst on rice by Brâhmans tasted,
  Lived my lord of handsome frame ;
Now he lives on forest produce,
  Thin and pale even like his fame !
On his feet, on jewels resting,
  Wreaths of kings their pollen dropped ;
Now they stray in forest jungle,
  By the deer or Brâhmans cropped.†

* Nakula and Sahadeva, the youngest of the Pândava brothers ;—Yudhishthira, Bhîma, and Arjuna being the elders.

† Brâhmans require the forest grass for their sacrifices.

And thy foes thy fall have compassed!
Thoughts like this my bosom rend;
Sufferings of unconquered heroes
Brighter glory on them lend! (41)

"Then spurn this sloth, assume thy prowess,
Dire destruction quick devise;
Hermits saintly, not proud monarchs,
Ever-during patience prize!
If great kings, whose wealth is glory,
Such great insult meekly bore,
Fame and chivalry be banished,
Honour's voice be heard no more!
If forgiveness thou wilt cherish,
Quelling pride and noble ire,
Leave this bow of royal glory,
Plait thy locks and worship fire!
Plighted faith with faithless foemen
Should not fetter thee for shame!
Artful monarchs bent on conquests
Fasten on their foes the blame! (45)

"Fettered by oath, and pale through glory lost,
Of power bereft, on seas of troubles tossed,
Arise, O king! thy mighty foemen quell,
As wakes the sun, night's darkness to dispel!"
(46)

BOOK II.

YUDHISHTHIRA'S REPLY.

LISTENING to her speech so noble,—
Speech with force and sweetness graced,
Bhîma thus with words of wisdom
Virtuous Yudhishthir addressed. (1)

"Pleading with her eyes so gentle,
Drupad's noble daughter speaks
Words unmatched by god of wisdom,—
And my soul in wonder wakes!
Easy steps can lead to knowledge,
As the *Ghat* leads to the stream;
Few are those in graceful accents
Who those easy steps can frame!
Like some potent drug her utterance
Force and mighty vigour blends;
Though displeasing to the weakly,
Still it serveth mighty ends!
May her words of noble import
Please thee, great and virtuous lord!
Wise men cull each word of wisdom,
Do not reck who speaks that word.

Trained in all the fourfold science
  Is thy lofty mind, great sire!
Wherefore then it sinks in error
  Like a tusker in the mire? (6)

"Fallen to this state deploréd,
  Mighty sovereign! can it be?
And thy power, by gods admiréd,
  Can it, monarch! sink with thee?
We may brook a foeman's prowess
  While his ruin we devise;
But a foeman's fall is painful
  If it leads to future rise!
Striving still their foes to conquer,
  And to seize the victor's prize,
Men of deeds and mighty valour
  Fate's reverses still despise!
Who in danger and misfortune
  From great deeds of daring turn;
Fortune shuns such nerveless monarchs,
  Moved by hatred, moved by scorn!
Who in danger and misfortune
  With their daring onward press,
Fortune helps them in the struggle,
  Men their mighty valour bless!
Righteous laws and rules of duty,
  They can lead to wealth and state;
But they wait on earnest effort,
  As we still depend on fate.
Men of deeds and men of honour,
  Bent on lofty aims with pride,

Still rely on man-like effort,
  Death and danger turn aside!
Men of feeble hearts surrender
  To the ills which fortune brings;
Lost their glory, lost their future!
  Lost their pride and state of kings! (14)

"Then spurn this apathy and weakness,
  To our fame a fatal bar;
On our effort, not vain sorrow,
  Ever waits fair fortune's star!
Waitest thou for term of treaty?
  Will the wicked wily foe,
Feasting long on royal splendour,
  Peacefully their state forego?
Waitest thou to get from foemen
  As a gift thy kingdom then?
Woe unto our might and prowess,
  Shame on us, O king of men!
Proud, the monarch of the forest
  Feeds on tuskers by him slayed!
Mighty chiefs who quell this wide earth
  Seek not gifts and foemen's aid!
They surrender life that fleeteth
  For undying glory great;
Fortune, fickle as the lightning,
  Will unchanging on them wait!
Men will spurn a heap of ashes,
  Not the bright and flaming fire!
Hence the proud their life surrender,
  Not their glory, not their ire!

Wherefore roars the forest-monarch,
  Till his roar the clouds repeat?
His proud soul will brook no rival,
  Mighty hearts know no defeat!
Set thy heart on glory, brother!
  Spurn this slothful life of shame,
Sure, from our inglorious weakness
  Springs our foeman's mighty fame!
Let thy brothers, strong as tuskers,
  In the dubious battle throng,
Who will face their mighty valour,
  Who will face their prowess strong?
And the fire the foes have lighted,—
  Making drear thy righteous life,—
Let the tears of foemen's widows
  Quench that great, that vengeful grief!" (24)

Bhîma, like a noble tusker,
  Spoke in wrath and mighty ire;
But the righteous Yudhishthira
  Strove to quench the flaming fire. (25)

"Wise thy reasons, noble brother,
  Blameless, mighty as thy might!
In thy words thy mind reflected
  Shines as on a mirror bright!
Strong thy sense, unveiled by jargon,
  Import deep yet manifest!
And thy purpose put forth nobly,
  And by native vigour graced!

Reasons urged with force inviolate,
Depth of lore unsoiled by art!
Who can speak so well and nobly
But a chief of noble heart?
But insatiate yet my bosom
Seeks for reason's holy light;
And thy wealth of precepts, brother,
Fails to teach me what is right! (29)

"Thoughtless action leads to evil,
And our dangers *we* create;
Fortune ever waits on wisdom,
On the wise her favours wait!
Sprinkle Wisdom's drops that nourish
On our Duty's fruitful seed,
And as autumn brings its harvests,
Duty will to glory lead!
Sacred lore bedecks a mortal,
Righteous peace befits our lore;
Prowess dwells in righteous conduct,
Leads to glory evermore!
On the wise man's path of duty,
When doubt's gloomy shadows lower,
Sacred lore then sheds a radiance
Like a lamp of wondrous power!
Dost thou cherish lofty purpose?
Righteously let it be done!
Dangers then will bring no sorrow,
Failure will be glory won!
Dost thou sigh for mighty conquests?
Angry passions lay aside!

Blamelessly thy ends pursue,
  And by blameless means abide!
Dost thou seek to rise in glory?
  Quell by wisdom passion's gloom;
As the sun quells impure darkness
  Ere he rises in his bloom!
Till thou quellest impure passions,
  Vain thy prowess, vain thy might,
Where is bright moon's silver glory
  In the dark and moonless night?
Act with pride and strength when needed,
  Or thy gentleness display;
Lord of passions,—rule the wide earth,
  Like the glorious orb of day!
But if thou be'st passions' minion,
  Fame nor glory wilt thou find,—
Fortune, fleeting as the white clouds,
  Favours not the inconstant mind. (39)

"Wherefore, brother, doth thy great heart
  This untimely wrath display?
Deep as the ocean is the bosom,
  Strong and firm be reason's sway!
Men who, versed in noble learning,
  Fail their passions to repress,—
They, my brother, to Dame Fortune,
  Give a name for fickleness!
Times nor means are ready, brother,
  Let not thy untimely wrath
Still inflame thee, like the vulgar,
  Nor mislead from duty's path!

Patience brightens up our future,
  Crowns our efforts with success,
Moves obstruction from our path,
  Leads us unto happiness! (43)

"The mighty chiefs of Yadu's race,*
  Who yield the foremost place to none,
Will not in their love forsake us,
  Will not bow to Suyodhan.†
Other friends and loving kinsmen
  Follow as the Yadus lead;
Not for love they serve Suyodhan,
  But to serve their present need.
If against our plighted treaty
  Now we fall upon the foe,
All the chiefs will round him gather,
  Like the flowers at morning's glow.
Grant them time, and all the chieftains
  Will the proud Suyodhan leave,
Chiefs will never brook those insults,
  Which his subjects often grieve.
For the pride of haughty monarchs,
  Scarcely trained in virtue's path,
Ill concealed by sense of duty,
  Oft breaks out in native wrath!
And the king with pride inflated
  Ever stoops to sin and folly;
Shuns the righteous path of wisdom
  As we shun the path unholy. (49)

* Allies of the Pâṇḍavas. Krishna was the chief of the Yadus, and ruled in Gujrat.

† A name of Duryodhana.

"A people's discontent will shake
 A mighty monarch's power and throne,
Till like a tree by tempest moved,
 With ease his rule is overthrown.
For people's discontent, though small,
 Doth wreck a mighty monarch's rule,
As far-extending woods are burnt
 By sparks which from a dead branch spring.
Therefore, brother, we endure
 A haughty foeman's sudden rise;
His haughtiness will sap his prowess,
 And his fall is like his rise!
By pride estranged, he soon is left
 By mighty chiefs and men of rank;
Then comes the foe and overwhelms him
 As the waves the loosened bank!" (53)

Thus spake the king unto his brother,—
 Wise and peaceful counsel lent;
When lo! approached,—like peace incarnate,—
 Holy Vyâsa,*—mighty saint!
His gentle look imparting love
 To every being animate;
His gentle visage softly beaming
 With a sin-destroying might!
Destroyer of all mortal sins,
 The source of every holy rite,
The saint appeared, serene and calm,
 Like virtue in its native might!

* The reputed compiler of the Vedas.

Attired in wild and ruddy barks,
  The king respectful stood, and shone,
As on Sumeru's lofty peaks
  Doth shine the ruddy rising sun!
And when was done obeisance meet,
  The king resumed his wonted place,
And shone as shines our sacred learning,
  Graced by righteous holy peace! (58)

His beauteous lips bedecked with beaming smile,
The monarch sat before the saint awhile,
And shone in splendour, like the full moon bright,
With Brihaspati in conjunction sweet! (59)

BOOK III.

VYÂSA'S INSTRUCTIONS.

Beaming with a gentle lustre
  Soft as rays of autumn night,
Graced with auburn locks that clustered
  Like a cloud with lightning bright!
Bearing grace in all its fulness
  On his more than mortal form,
Filling every living creature
  With affection pure and warm!
Speaking by his gentle features
  Peaceful thoughts that filled his heart,
By his soft and trustful glances
  Seeking confidence t' impart!
Mighty source of all the Vedas,
  Source from whom all virtues flow,
Him the King Yudhishthir questioned,
  Curious his great end to know. (4)

"Unattained by mighty virtue,
  Saint! thy visit is to me
Like a holy life's fruition,
  Like the rain from cloudless sky!
Rites performed bear fruit to-day,
  Brâhmans' blessings bring forth weal,

Mighty Saint! since by thy visit
  Honoured in this world I feel!
By its grace it conquers evils,
  By its glory spreads our fame,
From thy kindness as from Brahmâ's,
  Untold bliss and blessings come!
Not the moon with gentle radiance
  Cheers my sad and weary eye,—
Now my heart forgets its sadness,
  Beats with joy, for thou art nigh!
Thy desire I may not question,
  Peaceful souls have no desires!
But a wish to hear thy utterance
  With a boldness me inspires!" (9)

In graceful words thus spoke the monarch;
  Vyâsa, by his kindness led,
Anxious for the monarch's glory,
  Thus unto Yudhishthir said: (10)

"He who strives for fame and glory
  Bears for all an equal love,
He who strives for peace and virtue
  Should with love impartial move.
Yet my partial heart, O monarch,
  Is by virtues drawn to thee;
Virtues have a power attractive
  Even on holy saints and high.
Are ye not of race imperial,
  Worthier far than Suyodhan?

Has the old king lost his reason *
  Thus to wrench from you your own?
And will fortune help a monarch
  Who on Karna places trust?
Friendship with unrighteous mortals
  Is but fame and honour lost!
When your foes left paths of virtue,
  You in virtue took your rest;
And midst changes, still unchanging,
  Shewed forgiveness, ever blest!
Vainly did they seek to shame thee,
  Man of ever changeless love!
'Tis thy wealth of worth and virtue
  In true light their actions prove!
But mark my words! by valour only
  You can win in battle's hour;
And in might is strong the foeman,—
  Therefore seek increase in power. (17)

"Jamadagni's son,† who conquered
  Thrice seven times the kings of earth,
Great though he, the chieftain trembles
  At great Bhîshma's ‡ mightier worth!

* Duryodhana's father, who banished the Pândava brothers after they had staked and lost their kingdom.

† Parasurâma, a Brâhman and son of Jamadagni, is said to have conquered and slaughtered the Kshatriyas twenty-one times. The struggle for supremacy which went on for centuries between the priests and kings of India (as in Europe in the Middle Ages) is darkly indicated in Parasurâma's story.

‡ Bhîshma, a great-uncle of Yudhishthira and Duryodhan alike, was the mightiest of the mighty warriors among the Kurus. He is said to have been safe from death except by his own will.

Death is powerless, death is conquered
 By that chief's resistless power;
Trembles earth when mighty Bhîshma
 Wields his bow in battle's hour!
Doughty Drona! * in the battle,
 Speeding arrows in his ire,
Like a world-consuming furnace
 With its quivering tongues of fire!
Fiery Karna † learnt his lessons
 From great Jamadagni's son.
Death himself, in Karna's presence
 Owns a terror, strange, unknown!
These are chiefs, believe me, monarch,
 Whom in battle thou shalt face!
Hence let Arjun with due penance
 Seek celestial arms and grace.
Let him seek that gift of prowess
 Gods themselves by penance crave,—
This, O monarch, is my mission,—
 Win the gift that speeds the brave." (23)

Then the great and mighty Arjun
 Stept forth reverent and slow,
Bowing to Yudhishthir's mandate,
 Like a student meek and low.

* Drona, a Brâhman, and preceptor of the Pândavas and of Duryodhana in arms. He was famed for forming phalanxes in battle.

† Karna, king of Anga or East Behar, was a fiery and wild chief, and was favoured by Duryodhana, because he was the only warrior among the princes of the age who was a match for Arjuna in archery and skill of arms.

And the gift, the fiery *mantra*,
  Issuing from the holy saint,
As the sunlight falls on lotus,
  So unto great Arjun went!
And the *mantra's* sacred radiance,
  Which the hero proudly wore,
Quickly oped his eye of reason,
  Taught him secrets of deep lore!
And his form betokened glory,
  And his heart was fixed and strong,
Urging penance pure and holy,
  Vyâsa spoke to Arjun young. (27)

"Strengthened by this *mantra*, Arjun!
  Yielding thy own place to none,
Girt in arms perform thy penance,
  Unto fasts, ablutions prone.
Let this Yaksha lead thee, youth!
  To the lofty golden hill,—
There you do your sacred penance,
  Please great Indra, do his will." (29)

Thus speaking to the mighty chief
  The saint evanished from his view,
Obedient to his sacred word
  Appeared the Yaksha, faithful, true.
The Yaksha bowed and felt a love
  For Arjun, gentle in his speech;
The pure are quick in confidence,
  And friendship is not far to reach. (31)

As darkness fills Sumeru's bowers
When slow the god of day departs,
The parting from the mighty Arjun
Filled with grief his brothers' hearts.
Dispelled awhile by sense of duty,—
Albeit so strong was brothers' love,—
The sorrow of the parting brothers,
Though keen, did not oppressive prove.
And hope and trust in Arjun's might,
And bitter hatred of the foe,
And confidence in Arjun's power
Dispelled the brothers' common woe.
As darkness leaves the hours of day
And seeks the stillness of the night,
Thus sorrow left the mighty chiefs,
And fell on Krishnâ * in its might.
As flakes of snow the lotus fills
Spontaneous tear-drops filled her eye,
Nor could she weep, for tear-drops shed
Might be an inauspicious sign!
One look she gave, 'twas dear to soul,—
And Arjun caught the parting grace,—
His treasure and memento dear
Through pathless woods and weary days.
By grief her tender heart was wrung,
Like summer rills by tuskers soiled;
Her voice was choked with tears restrained,
She spoke in accents sweet and wild. (38)

* Krishnâ (with a long *â*) is a name of Draupadi. Krishna (with a short *a*) is the name of the Yâdava chief, the ally of the Pândavas.

"Restorer of our ancient fame,
Now trailed in mire by foemen's art,
Until thy mighty penance ends,
Our absence should not pain thy heart.
In fame's pursuit, in pleasure's quest,
In deeds which glorious records fill,
Unfailing Fortune leans to him
Who labours with a mighty will :
To rule the world was Kshatriya made,
His wealth is conquering power in strife !
Disgrace, alas ! has quenched that power,—
To true-born warriors dear as life !
Disgrace, which kings in distant lands
Have doubting heard, heads bent in shame !
Which stains our former stainless worth,
Our world embracing mighty fame !
Disgrace, which wipes our former deeds,
And hides in gloom our glory's blaze !
Which wipes our future prospects fair,
As evening wipes the sun's last rays !
Disgrace by hated foemen dealt,—
This bitter thought is cruel, smart !
Disgrace which in thy absence, chief !
Will freshen in this sorrowing heart. (44)

"How changed thou art ! like wounded tuskers,
Prowess lost, and glory faded,
Deprived of power by foemen's wile,
Like day by clouds of autumn shaded !
Thy arms unused have lost their glow,
Nor deck thee as they did of yore ;

Thy form how changed, like summer lakes,
  Now faded by the loss of power!
Duhsâsan dragged me by this hair!
  Untied they are, their lord is fate!
On thy great fame they cast reproach,
  Oh! art thou Dhananjay * the great?
A Kshatriya he who can protect—
  A bow is useful in the war—
But vain their import if they fail
  In virtues by their name they bear.
Thy warlike virtues, all but dead,
  Ingloriously thy rise await,
And seem to share our common grief,
  And imitate our common plight! (49)

"But rash thy foemen thee insult,
  As tuskers touch a lion's mane!
Duty for thy worth elects thee,
  As the day elects the sun!
A hero's deeds all deeds excel,
  And fill the glorious rolls of fame;
A hero's name holds foremost place
  When men their mighty chieftains name!
Then be a hero! do thy deeds,—
  And if perchance within thy heart,
A thought of us awakes a pang,
  May Indra every grief avert!
In sacred spots, from dangers free,
  May all thy time in safety pass;

* A name of Arjuna. Duhsâsana, a brother of Duryodhana, dragged Draupadî by the hair after Yudhishthira had lost his kingdom. Draupadî declined to braid her hair after that till that insult was revenged.

Beware the wicked, impure foes
  Who turn against the pure, alas!
Thy duty calls thee! Arjun, go!
  Perform the saint's behest in peace;
And all our dearest hopes fulfilling,
  Come thou to our dear embrace!" (54)

Thus spoke Drupad's noble daughter,
  Deepening his resentment high;
And he crimsoned in his anger
  Like the sun in northern sky!
Accoutred in his mighty weapons,
  Fancying all his foes before,
As spells assume a power terrific,
  He a form terrific wore!
The bow before which foemen trembled,
  Famed by many a mighty deed,
The quivers never seen by foemen,
  And the long and shining blade,
And his gem-bespangled armour,
  Like the star-decked sky,—he wore!
Scars by Indra's darts inflicted,
  Hid by glory evermore!
Guided by the faithful Yaksha
  He unto the mountains hied,
Filled the hearts of saints with sorrow,
  As with tears the chief they eyed. (59)

A heavenly music filled the realms on high,
And fragrant blossoms gently fell from sky,
And the sea with breakers ever restless
Clasped the earth to whisper words of sweetness! (60)

BOOK IV.

AUTUMN FIELDS.

Now Arjun came to peopled lands,
 All fresh and blooming as a bride ;
The tuneful birds flew in the sky,
 The crops were rich in golden pride !
And autumn's charms, before him spread,
 A scene of beauty seemed to make ;
The corn that bent with golden ears,
 The winding path, the lotus lake !
And fish whose glancing movements stole
 The beauty of a woman's glance ;
And lakes whose lotus blossoms seemed
 Like eyes uplifted in a trance !
And stretching fields of growing rice
 Still standing on a watery sheet,
Where oft the lily raised its head,—
 Beauteous things harmonious met !
So still the water, pollen decked,
 On land the lilies seemed to grow,
Until some glancing fish disturbed
 The sweet illusion of the show !
And Arjun saw the beauteous sands,
 All pure and white as unstained sheet,

And marked with waving lines by water,
  Receding in the autumn's heat! (6)

The rustic maid upon her locks
  The scarlet blossom placed with pride;
Her eyebrows caught the pollen dust,
  Her bright red lips its colour vied!
And bright she stood in morning's light,
  And wore a lotus on her breast;
Her skin was moist with honest toil,
  And fragrant with the lotus dust!
And on her ears she hung two lilies,
  Sweet as glances from her eye;
And Arjun in her saw the charms
  Of autumn in their full display! (9)

The lowing herds returned from fields,
  Where they had grazed the previous night;
Their eagerness to meet their calves,
  Their streaming udders pleased his sight!
Fed in autumn's pastures rich,
  The bull victorious in the fight,
Bellowing, breaking banks of rivers,
  Seemed,—incarnate form of might!
Slowly from the banks of rivers
  Herds of snow-white cows withdrew,
As if the beauteous silver streams
  White garments from their persons drew.
With brother's love their cattle tending,
  In woods a home's affections bearing,
The cow-herds lived among the cattle,
  All their simple habits sharing! (13)

The village maiden churned the milk,—
  Her face was like the lotus fair,
Her teeth were like its beauteous leaves,
  Like restless bees oft moved her hair!
She held her breath, her red lips moved,
  And like a creeper soft she stood,
And gently moved her beauteous frame
  As with her hands she turned the rod!
A deep sound from the vessel rose,
  Still as the churning rod went round;
The startled pea-hen in the yard
  Half thought it was the thunder's sound!
With toil her heaving bosom throbbed,
  And languid was her eye's soft glance,
And thus she vied in rustic beauty
  Courtly maidens at a dance! (17)

He went by paths no longer winding,
  Through the crops by cattle eaten;
The thickened mud was marked by cart wheels,
  And by steps the path was beaten.
Beauteous as a saint's retreat
  He saw the rustic homesteads smile,
Where, simple in their thoughts and ways,
  The rustics lived by honest toil.
Thus autumn's varied charms to scan,
  With gladdened eyes pleased Arjun sought;
With gladdened heart the Yaksha spoke,
  Reading his companion's thought. (20)

"This cloudless time with crystal waters,
  Comes the tiller's toil to bless;

Like a happy life's fruition,
  May it bring to thee success!
The corn assumes its golden hue,
  The streams are clear, the earth is dry;
From charms the rainy time displays,
  To autumn's fresher charms we fly!
What though no white cranes deck the sky,
  Nor are the skies with rainbows graced;
The autumn sky hath beauty rare,
  And beauty unadorned is best!
What though the god of rains is gone,
  Nor lightnings deck the clouds now pale;
Like sorrowing wives the autumn clouds
  In paler grace are lovely still!
What though the peacock's loveless notes *
  Are loud and harsh, nor please the ear;
The loving notes of autumn songsters
  To the lover's heart are dear!
What golden crops,—rich in their beauty,
  With their load of ears bent low!
They bend as if to feel the fragrance
  Of the flowers that spring below!
What beauteous lakes,—green with their plants,
  And scarlet with the lotus bloom,
And golden with the ripened corn,
  Like molten rainbow varied seem!
What nymph-like groves,—they smile in flowers,
  And in the blue buds ope their eyes,

* The rains are supposed to be the season of love for peacocks. Hence peacocks hear the sound of thunder with delight and joy; and after the rains their note is loveless and harsh.

And lotus dust by zephyrs driven
Clothe them in a fairy dress!
What snow-white clouds make cool the day,
In balmy skies no lightning lowers;
How cool the breeze with watery spray,
How sweet with fragrance from the flowers!
Above, the happy white-winged birds
Are flying, twittering as they fly!
Or are the quarters of the heavens
Holding converse in the sky? (30)

"From the rich autumnal pastures,
Eager to their village home,
Sweet milk from their udders streaming,
How the cows to young ones come!
Noble, gentle, tender beings,
Nourishers of the humankind!
How the mothers join their young ones,—
Like sweet hymns to offerings joined!
Blithe the song the milkmaid singeth,
Sweet as strains the Kokils weave!
How entranced yon herd of antlers,
Listen,—and their pastures leave!
In the lakes the reeds are bending,
As to court yon lotus fair!
But disdainful is that beauty,
Pale the reeds with chill despair!
Sweet the breeze with lotus pollen,
Saturate with cooling spray;
And like giddy thoughtless men
Yon wind-blown bee has lost his way!

How beauteous green yon flight of birds,
Their beaks in glorious crimson shine;
How golden is the corn they bear,
Is it a checkered rainbow's line?"
While thus he spoke, before him stood,
Concealing the bright god of day,
Like fleecy clouds in masses piled,
The towering range of Himalay! (37)

Darksome forests in his valleys spread,
But snow eternal graced his lofty head!—
He seemed the god, who wears a dusky dress,
Who holds the plough, and wears a ruddy face.* (38)

* Baladeva, holder of the plough, fair in complexion, and often ruddy with the flush of wine.

BOOK V.

THE HIMALAYAS.

THE towering Himalaya rose,
  Surpassing mighty Meru high,
To view the limits of wide space,
  Perchance to scale the lofty sky!
Eternal sunshine on his face,
  His back in ceaseless gloomy night,
Like Siva in dark tusker-skin,
  His face with radiant smiles all bright!
Dwellers of earth and sky and heaven
  Mutually unseen here dwell;
This range, itself a perfect world,
  Displaying Sambhu's mighty skill!
All white the heaven-kissing peaks,
  With glittering gold the plateaus streaked,
And bright as autumn's fleecy clouds
  With golden glittering lightning decked!
Like peopled towns the mountain plateaus
  Streaked with gems which silk-like beam,
And creeper grots by nymphs frequented
  Which like sylvan dwellings seem!
Aloft, the rainless, sparkless clouds,
  In white and fleecy masses piled,
Are like the mountain's giant wings,
  Far-extending, vast and wild! (6)

Wild tuskers gore the rocky banks,
  Which many a costly mine conceal;
And sacred rills their waters pour,
  Which every pious wish fulfil!
And mountain gems shine with a ray,
  As of the soft-hued crimson flower,
And shed o'er plateaus, streaked with gold,
  The chastened light of evening hour!
Untold Kadambas grace the scene,
  The Tamal lends its cooling shade,
And mighty tuskers range the wood
  Where melting snow falls in cascade! *
In priceless gems the peaks are rich,
  The vales with beauteous creepers blessed;
Wild torrents flow through flowery banks,
  And trees are with wild blossoms graced!
And mountain nymphs bedecked in gold
  Oft frolic in the sparkling rills;
And Nâgas, fond of trees and creepers,
  Love to dwell in wooded hills.
And fleecy clouds with rainbow graced
  Oft rest the gem-decked peaks around,
And seem like snowy mountain peaks
  Until ye hear the thunder's sound! (12)

* This verse, like many other verses of this Book, is, in the original, unsurpassed in the beauty of its alliteration. But the beauty of his verse serves to veil the poet's somewhat imperfect knowledge of the scenes he describes! Mountain gems do not in their native state shine with the lustre of silk or of flowers or of the evening; streaks of gold are not seen on the surface of plateaus; the Kadamba and the Tamal trees do not grow in the higher latitudes of the Himalayas; and wild tuskers do not range in the latitudes where the melting snow falls in cascades!

Sweet-voiced ducks and lilies grace
  Pure Mânasa! thy waters cool,
Where Umâ often meets her lord,
  Begirt by troops, but calm in soul!
And oft his worshippers recall
  Tripurâ burnt by Siva's ire,
When lighting planets in the sky
  Flames forth at night the forest fire!
And rolling down from mighty plateaus,
  Spreading in a mass of spray,
And winding through deep rocky gorges,
  Gangâ shines like Châmar* gay!
And Arjun's mind was struck with wonder
  At this great, this glorious sight;
And unto him thus spoke the Yaksha,
  Words appropriate, soft and sweet. (16)

"Sacred range! whose snow-white turrets
  Pierce the lofty vault of heaven,
Sinful mortals view these mountains,
  And their sins are all forgiven!
Its deeper parts like Brahmâ's Self,
  In sacred Sâstras faintly told,
Are unto mortals all unknown,—
  The outer ranges they behold!
Here creeper grots are rich in flowers,
  And lucid lakes in lilies blown;
And haughty nymphs, wooed by their swains,
  A sweet and soft emotion own!

* Fan made of the snow-white tail of the mountain yak.

And aye, this mountain fills the earth
With wealth above all worlds, I ween,
And mortals by Kuvera's gift *
Their dearest wishes here obtain!
The wealth of all the worlds combined
The sacred Himalay excels,
For here in grace and power divine
Great Sambhu with his Umâ dwells!
Who freed from sins and mortal life
Seek Brahmâ's holy mansion pure,
They seek it here in contemplation,
As in Sâstra's sacred lore! (22)

"Oft in these vales celestial footprints,
Garlands cast away and pale,
And beds of flowers in sweet disorder,
Tales of secret love they tell!
And on these hills by worlds adored
The plant at night its flame gives forth,†
As glory shines on virtuous kings
Attained by might and pious worth!
And in the groves which bend with flowers
His lay the sweet-voiced Kokil trills,
And tuskers feed on watery plants
Beside the cool and shaded rills!
And oft they rub their scented heads
Upon the gnarléd forest tree,
The mango scent excites the Kokil,
And attracts the maddened bee!

* God of wealth, supposed to live in the Himalayas.

† Certain plants growing in the mountains are supposed to emit a light by night.

Beside these sweetly sounding rills
  Celestial maidens often rove,
And drink the drink of gods,—the nectar,
  Which the gods and Nâgas love!
And as they rest in creeper grots,
  And soft the gentle breeze sweeps by,
Faint with love's toil, they feel its charm,
  Nor seek their homes in upper sky! (28)

"Here sweet-eyed Umâ sought her lord.
  By rites and penance duly made;
And Siva here in love's sweet tremor
  Clasped the blushing mountain maid!
Gods and Asurs, for the nectar.
  Erst with Mandâr churned the sea,*
Bearing still the serpent's trail,
  Here Mandâr scales the lofty sky!
And crystal rocks in masses piled
  Reflect the red sun's radiant beams,
And chastened by the sapphires blue
  The day like softer moonlight seems.
And on the ripples of the lake,
  As sweet as woman's flashing eye,
The lotus bud is gently moved
  By gentle zephyrs from the sky! (32)

"When sweet-eyed Umâ gave her hand
  To Siva by these mountain lakes,

* The nectar was obtained from the sea, churned by the gods and the Asuras. The hill Mandâra was the churning rod, and the great serpent allowed himself to be used as a rope to turn the rod with!

Her hand was twined with sacred grass,
  And Siva's hand was twined with snakes!
And crystal rocks with sunbeams lit
  Sent forth a bright and dazzling ray,
And heightened more the light of sun
  And beautified the sacred day!
And on Kailâsa's lofty peak,
  Round which revolves th' unwearied sun,
To please great Siva, lord of hosts,
  Kuvera built his beauteous town!
There sparkling rays of crystal rocks
  In brilliant tints harmonious blend,
And to the eye of the beholder
  Strange delusions often lend!
Eternal verdure decks the fields,
  The soft green woods enchant the view,
And trees with blossoms ever crowned
  Nor fade nor wear the yellow hue!
The emerald's rays, like fresh green grass,
  Deceive and tempt the forest deer,
And with a soft and chastened radiance
  Mingle with the sunbeams clear! *
And the pollen from the blossoms,
  Wafted from the flowering trees,
Like a golden canopy
  Floats upon the evening breeze! (39)

* We are afraid our friend the Yaksha is taking a somewhat undue advantage of Arjuna's credulity and faith! Sapphires in their native state scarcely turn the day into moonlight by their azure glow; crystal rocks scarcely delude the eye; and the forest deer is too knowing to mistake for grass such emeralds as may lie on the surface of the rocks. But the indulgent reader will make allowance for the Yaksha's "local patriotism," or his poetic fire!

"Oft at early dawn are seen
Unequal footprints by the rills,
For Umâ with the mighty Siva
Loves to haunt these sacred hills!
And oft at noon, through leafy trees,
The day-god's struggling, radiant beam
Strikes on the bright and crystal rock,
And makes it like a mirror gleam!
And oft at night, on distant peaks,
Great Siva's snow-white bull is seen,
And wondering females gaze and ask,
Is it the full-orbed rising moon?
What though the rainbow's broken arch
On fleecy clouds is faint and pale,
Borrowing fulness from the gems
It bends sublime o'er rock and vale!
What though the gloom in moonless nights
O'ershadows valley, hill and lea,
The moon on Siva's ample crest
Pours forth a light on flower and tree! (44)

"Yonder hill with golden caverns
Is to mighty Indra dear;
How its peaks with golden lustre
Woods and spreading forests cheer!
And oft when mountain breezes blow,
And move luxuriant creepers thick,
The golden beams of that bright hill
Even like the flashing lightning break!

Celestial tuskers range that hill,
  And shake the scented Chandan tree; *
Before their might all earthly creatures
  In their terror turn and flee!
And sapphires here with azure tints
  Make soft the sun's effulgent ray;
And darksome clouds in glorious masses
  Temper here the light of day! (48)

"There Kshatriya-like thy penance do,
  As by the saintly Vyâsa told;—
By noble efforts, constant toil,
  Achieve their fame the great and bold!
May Siva grant thee strength and might,
  Bestow on thee his blessed grace;
And be the gods thy constant help,
  And bless thy labours with success!"
Thus spoke, and hied unto his home
  The Yaksha, gentle, kind, and good;
And Arjun pensive saw him part,
  And for a moment sorrowing stood. (51)

He reached the hill, uncrossed by living wight,
With luscious fruits and blossoms on its height;
And as he gazed upon the lofty hill,
Great thoughts of noble deeds his heart did fill! (52)

* The Chandana is the Sandal tree. Elephants and snakes are supposed to be fond of this tree.

BOOK VI.

ARJUNA'S PENANCE.

ARJUN, on his penance bent,
  Followed Gangâ's rocky course,
Scaled the hill, as Vishnu * mounts,
  The golden bird which heavenward soars.
Forest trees like worshippers
  Sang his praise with hum of bees,
Bent their heads and rained their blossoms,
  Gently shaken by the breeze!
And the sweet and scented zephyrs,
  Saturate with Gangâ's spray,
Softly blew on Arjun's forehead,
  And embraced him in their play!
And the roar of wild cascades,
  Wafted o'er the woodland hum,
And the notes of forest birds
  Stirred him like the beat of drum! (4)

Cascades and rapid mountain torrents
  Sweep the tall trees in their course,
But the gentle bending creeper
  Escapes their wild resistless force.

* Vishnu, with Brahmâ and Siva, forms the Trinity of the Hindu religion. The golden Garuda, like Jupiter's eagle, is Vishnu's favourite bird.

And tuneful ducks before him fly,
  And with their voices fill the brake,
In burnished gold swim on the waves,—
  A golden mantle on the lake!
In deepest wilds the tuskers roam,
  And mark the banks with many a scar;
The swarming bees fly to the spot,
  And streaming moisture scents the air!
The golden Chakravâk is lost
  Midst waves in golden tints that shine,
And Arjun hears the tender female
  Call her mate in gentle tone!
Varying tints upon the stream
  Proclaim the gems in rocks below,
As colours on the changeful face
  The workings of the mind oft show.
But oft the surges, lashed by wind,
  Spread far and wide their foam awhile,—
White as Ketak's snowy flower,—
  Brightening the woods with their bright smile!
But mark those spots, like peacock's feather,
  Floating on the lucid wave;
Wild elephants their juice exude,
  As they within the waters lave.
And Arjun views the yawning oysters,
  Lying on their sandy bed,
Beauteous with their glistening pearls,*
  Or are they tears in sorrow shed?

* Like many an enthusiastic modern traveller, Arjuna must have had a lively imagination to discover pearl-oysters in Himalayan lakes!

The creeper's crimson budding shoot,
  Which oft the snowy dewdrop tips,
Recalls unto the lover's mind
  His nymph's fair teeth, her maddening lips!
And tuskers gambol in the wave,
  And frolic in the streamlets fair;
The waters own their mighty lords,
  And odours scent the loaded air!
But often from the placid lake
  The coily snake darts in the air,
And breathes its poisoned breath in bubbles
  White as clouds in autumn fair. (15)

Arjun many a streamlet crossed,—
  With fishes, bright as woman's eye,—
Like maidens waiting on their queen,
  The streamlets to great Gangâ hie!
And then he scaled the towering hill,
  And found a spot, alone, apart,
Begirt by many a flowering tree,
  And pure as purity of heart!
The creepers decked with forest flowers,
  And trees where fruits in clusters hung,
Inclined great Arjun's pious heart
  To pious rites and penance long.
By rules ordained he fixed his heart
  On penance which the saintly know;—
What though the penance was severe,
  Who conquers self can feel no woe.
He quelled his passions by his will,
  Dispelled all sins by virtue's light,

And rose in merit day by day
Like waxing moon of autumn night.
All thoughts and cravings of the flesh
By contemplation were dispelled,
Until a righteous holy peace
Great Arjun's saintly bosom filled.
By holy hymns and worship due
He sought the mighty King of skies,
And in his heart harmonious dwelt,
A lofty power,—a holy peace! (22)

He wore his plaited manlike locks
Red as anchorites should wear;
The tall tree wears its crest of leaves
Fringed by morning's red beams fair!
Begirt in arms!—but like great saints
In holy deed and gentle soul!
The forest creatures knew his love,
For love of heart endeareth all!
The breezes softly blew on him,
And shed a fragrance as it went;
The tropic sun forgot its heat,
And but a chastened radiance lent.
And when the hero plucked the flowers,
The stately tall trees bent their head;
The earth put forth her tender grass
To make the hero's nightly bed!
The cloudless sky auspicious sent
Untimely rain the dust to lay;
And kindly nature helped his toil,
And nursed the hero night and day.

The blossom of his glorious fate
  By laws divine its fruit thus bore;
But signs like these moved not his heart,
  The great are firm for evermore! (28)

Great Indra's menials in the forest
  Heard of Arjun's rites severe,
His mighty merit, lofty virtue,—
  To their monarch went in fear.
Before the monarch of the sky
  The menials their obeisance made,
And in a humble graceful speech
  Thus of the unknown hermit said. (30)

"Like a luminary of the sky,
  Though clad in barks, on yonder hill,
A man intent on purpose high
  Doth penances! And earth is still!
In arms, whose muscles snake-like coil,
  He holds a mighty powerful bow;
But gentle are his deeds and rites,
  No gentler hermit lives below.
The wind blows soft, the sward is green,
  And gentle rains the dust allay;
By worth subdued the elements
  In one accord obeisance pay.
The forest beasts their strife forget,
  And listen to his beck and word;
For him the trees with blossoms wait,
  The mountains own him as their lord!

His toil bespeaks a purpose high,
  His mien denotes success is near;
A gentle hermit! but his eye
  Instils a sense of secret fear!
If from great saints he counts descent,
  From Daityas sprung or kingly line,
We know not, Lord! Nor why in woods
  He penance doth and rites divine.
Perchance he toils for purpose high,
  Perchance it is our ignorance,
But as we feel, so speak we, Lord!
  We foresters are poor in sense!" (37)

Dear to Indra, what they told
  Of holy rites which Arjun did;
But wishing still his faith to try,
  His rising joy within him hid.
Awhile he thought; and then pretending
  Not to know great Arjun's mind,
He sought for means to try the saint,
  And to the nymphs spoke soft and kind. (39)

"Sweetly subtle, gently piercing,
  Heavenly nymphs! your eye's keen dart!
No arrow speedeth in its flight
  So true, unerring, to the heart!
For righteous lore seek anchorites
  To conquer sins and ills of life;
That potent lore, obtained by toil,
  Before your merry glance is weak!

All lovely things in universe,
  All beauteous form and winning charm,
Combine to shape your heavenly grace!
  Then wield that grace, the saint disarm!
Go forth with sweet musicians skilled,
  Destroy the mortal's useless rite;
Great anchorites have felt thy power,
  A youth will feel thy conquering might!
'Tis sure he seeks for joys of earth
  But by the conquest of his foe;
Who seeks for heaven strives not so,
  Who seeks for peace wields not the bow!
And dread not from a mighty warrior
  Curse, as from an anchorite;
For kind to females, full of sweetness
  Are great warriors in their might."
Honoured thus with high behest
  The nymphs bowed to great Indra's will,
And with a lovelier beauty shone,
  For honours heightened powers instil! (46)

The nymphs obeisance made, and slow retired,
With lovelier charms and pleasing hopes inspired;
And Indra with his lotus eyes gazed still
Upon their swelling charms, nor gazed his fill! (47)

BOOK VII.

THE NYMPHS.

THE beauteous nymphs then left the sky,
  Attended by Gandharvas skilled,
And joyous notes of drum and shell
  And sound of cars the blue vault filled.
And eager denizens of the sky
  Poured forth to greet them as they went;
The orb of day with upward beams
  Upon the nymphs his radiance lent.
The toil of the unwonted march,
  The blowing breeze, the sun's bright shine,
Crimsoned their blushing cheeks and brow
  As with the gentle flush of wine!
Celestial coursers fresh and powerful
  Drew the cars with speed of wind;
Scarce the wheels did seem to roll,
  But sky and space flew quick behind!
From regions far, close to the sun,
  Where his red rays are bright and strong,
Far far they went, where like a braid
  Celestial Gangâ rolls along.
Cooling zephyrs, gently blowing,
  Saturate with Gangâ's spray,

M

Scented by the heavenly lotus,
 Cheered the damsels on their way.
And in many a fold the clouds
 Spanned the space 'twixt earth and sky,
And the steeds by drivers checked
 Lighted on the earth from high.
The scented woods of Himalay,
 Blooming creepers, beauteous trees,
Hailed the heavenly nymphs with joy,
 Honoured by their matchless grace! (8)

And now the nymphs in quest of flowers
 Wandered through the woodland way,
Unheeding many a shrub and blossom,
 So thick the flowers, so merry they!
The maddened bee forsook the bush
 To cull the nectar from their arms;
Their pink white hands were like young shoots,
 Their fingers wore the blossom's charms!
Sweetly flowed the mountain rill,
 Her sands were robed with Kusa chaste,
And graceful strings of tuneful ducks
 Like chain of gold bedecked her waist!
Cascades in silver masses fell,
 And spread afar in ripples bright;
And all the wild woods seemed to smile
 With the spray so pearly white.
And creepers oped their gentle blossoms
 Decked with strings of dark blue bees,
Like tender-hearted gentle maidens
 With their soft and trustful eyes! (13)

All around the blossoms hung
  As through the woods the damsels moved,
With female art, for needless help,
  They asked the fond Gandharvas * loved.
Some nymph with lifted, blushing face,
  Still hung on soft tales whispered nigh ;
Her idle hand no blossom culled,
  The loosened robe forgot to tie!
Some with flower-buds decked her ringlets,
  With her beauteous tapering arms,
And scarce rebuked the loving swain
  Who gently clasped her swelling charms!
Some sought her lover's gentle aid
  To blow the pollen from her eye,
And scarce the lover could regret
  The sweet mishap that drew him nigh!
Laden with flowers the nymphs returned
  From flowering woods,—a merry band,
Their weary feet scarce knew the way,
  And often slipped on even land!
Their girdles rich in sparkling gems,
  Hung loose below their slender waist ;
The loosened zone proclaimed their languor,
  And their panting heaving breast!
Their velvet cheeks were dewed with toil,
  Like lotus dimmed with streaks of snow!
The gods in rapture viewed the nymphs,
  Their languid charms, their movements
      slow! (20)

* Celestial musicians, loved by the nymphs.

To Gangâ's sparkling cooling wave
The languid damsels slow repair;
Where fishes glance through lilies blown,
And notes of wild fowl fill the air.
The eager waters clasped the nymphs,
And played with garlands on their hair,
And rashly washed their Chandain paints,
In little wavelets fled afar!
Some damsel hid, and others searched,
Are those her eyes or lotus bright?
Is that her hair or string of bees?
Are those her teeth or lilies sweet?
Some nymph on others water threw,
Or washed and wet, yet lovelier shone!
Her face was flushed, her bosom heaved,
Scarce held her robe the loosened zone!
The sportive nymphs arose at last,
Like rain-washed lilies doubly bright,
Still sparkling with the glistening drops,
And radiant as the starry night! (25)

So closed the day, and darkness fell
O'er stream and forest, far and nigh,
And beauty left the things of earth
And shone upon the starry sky.
Until the brightening eastern heaven,
Streaked with silver, faintly shone,
And pure and white as Ketak flower
Spread the light of rising moon!
Slowly rolled the flood of light
O'er the dark and nightly sky,

Like the Gangâ's ruddy wave
  Mingling with the azure sea!
Like a disk of burnished gold,
  Flooding earth and sky with light,
From the distant eastern main
  Rose the glorious Lord of night!
And he drew the veil of gloom
  From the face of earth so wide,
As a kinsman draws the veil
  For to bless a bashful bride! (30)

At dawn the heavenly nymphs arose,
  Decked themselves with jewels rare;
Went to Arjun's hermitage
  With sweet glances, graces rare!
On their feet the tinkling bells,
  On their waists the sounding chain;
With soft music filled the woods
  Till the birds sang back the strain!
Pale with penances and rites,
  Clad in arms, but calm and great,
Peaceful as the mighty Vedas,
  Arjun great at last they met!
Radiant in a robe of light
  On the lofty hill he stood,
Like the beauteous lord of night
  Seemed the lord of all the wood!
Pale with penances,—but great,
  Warlike,—in his peaceful bower,
Alone,—but strong as hosts in war,
  A saint,—but wielding Indra's power! (35)

To him, more than mortals mighty,
Slow the artful damsels come,
Conscious of their matchless beauty,
Vain they know his rites and aim!
Slow and soft a music soundeth
Through the glades and o'er the hills;
Every season brings its blessings,
And the wood with rapture fills!
Round the hermitage of Arjun
Mâlatîs in blossoms grow;
Washed by rains the lotus blossoms
With a lovelier freshness blow!
On the luscious berries feasting
Kokils sing their joyous lay,
Gladdening e'en the mourner's bosom
With their wondrous melody!
Breezes blow through sweet Kadambas,
Wafting peacocks' notes of love,
Gently fanning pious Arjun
From his rites his heart to move!
Mango blossoms lend their fragrance,
Cooling zephyrs gently move,
Spring and winter move conjointly
Wakening gentle thoughts of love!
On the jasmine's opening blossoms.
Shaken by the gentle breeze,
Sweet as quivering lips of maidens,
Love's sweet kisses press the bees!
Jasmine sweet nor lilies scented
Ope so sweet, when darkness flies,

As upon the saintly Arjun
  Oped the nymphs their merry eyes! (43)

Before the saints the nymphs appear,
  And lightly step upon the grass;
Their tender feet vermilion painted
  On the heather gently press!
Some nymph behind her maid conceals—
  From coyness, or from female art,—
Her sidelong glance on Arjun sends,
  Betraying feelings of her heart!
Another frolics on the meadow
  In her blooming loveliness;
The wanton zephyrs oft disclose
  Her budding charms, bewitching grace!
Some damsel resteth on the green,
  On her fair hand her pale face raising,
And with her soft and languid eyes
  Upon the beauteous hero gazing.
Another sings with thirsty lips
  And frequent sighs some ancient lay,
And her soft eyes and heaving bosom
  Speak the words she cannot say!
Some sprightly nymph beside the tree
  From her sweet and laughing eyes
Sends on Arjun tender darts,
  Rapid as the arrow flies!
Another damsel scours the plain,
  Her loosened robes held on her breast
But scarce her nimble feet can move,
  The slipping zone restrains her haste!

But vain these blandishments and charms,
And vain each winning female art!
Still steadfast in its lofty faith,
Unmoved like rock is Arjun's heart! (51)

Attended by their swains the nymphs withdrew,
And Arjun, to his purpose ever true,
With pious rites, and faith, ennobling, high,
In prayers sought the Lord of earth and sky. (52)

BOOK VIII.

THE ADVENT OF INDRA.

ARJUN, mighty in his strength,
  All impure passions overcame;
And to his holy hermitage,
  Rejoiced at heart, great Indra came.
He came disguised,—as come the gods,—
  Even like an ancient anchorite,
Wearied by a tiresome journey,
  Weak in limbs and weak in sight.
And his crimson plaited locks
  Upon his white hair mingled fell,
As the evening's crimson radiance
  Mingles with the moonbeams pale.
All wrinkled with the mark of age,
  His eyes by fleecy eyebrows shaded,
Were like the lotus of the lake,
  Its petals by a snow-fall faded.
But his limbs, though very slender,
  Seemed instinct with strength and life;
Like an aged man and hoary,
  Nourished by a careful wife!
In feeble form concealed, great Indra
  Shone with more than mortal power;

The radiant sun is hidden faintly
  By a light and passing shower!
And a grace divine he wore,
  Albeit so ancient and so hoary,
And o'er the hills and woodlands spread
  The lustre of his shaded glory!
Prithâ's son * received the guest,
  And held him in a fond embrace;
True friends an unknown joy inspire,
  Albeit unknown to us their face!
And Indra, pleased at heart, received
  Obeisance which to guests is paid,
And rested on a mat of grass,
  In gentle accents thus he said. (9)

"Well hast thou in early age
  In these rites thy choice hast made;
Aged mortals like myself
  Oft by worldly things are led.
And thy penance, noble youth,
  Is endued with virtues fair,—
Handsome forms we often meet,
  Handsome virtues,—they are rare!
Transient as the autumn clouds,—
  Pride and pomp of humankind;
Pleasures please us for a day,
  Bitter sorrows leave behind!
Mortals' days are full of evils,
  Death cuts short our life's brief span;

* Arjuna's mother was Kuntî or Prithâ.

Therefore in this fleeting world
Virtue seeks the holy man.
Wise and nobly thou hast chosen
Holy rites to virtue dear,
But, belying thy great penance,
Thy attire fills me with fear! (14)

"Like a warrior, on thy mien
Wherefore wear'st this armour bright?
Skins and barks of forest trees
Suit the holy anchorite.
Void of earthly vain desires
In the virtuous path you go;
Wherefore, then, O noble youth!
Quivers and this mighty bow?
And by mortals ever feared,—
Death's right hand,—this mighty blade!
Doth it in thy holy rites
Unto peace thy feelings lead?
Sure against some mortal foe
War and triumph you must seek;
Weapons are designed for war,
In forgiveness dwell the meek!
He who sighs for warlike fame
Soils these rites and penance holy,
As the spring's pellucid water
Soils the fool who acts in folly.
Cherish not the lust of fame,
For it leads to sinful deeds,
Casts a stain on stainless rites,
And from peace our heart misleads. (20)

"He who strives with lust of glory,
Wins awhile a vile success,—
But as rivers end in oceans,—
So he ends in dire distress!
Wealth is won by evil measures,
And to evils leads each morrow,—
Wealth is but a name for trouble,
Leads to sufferings and to sorrow!
Impure pleasures, joys of earth,
Kill our peace and steadfast faith,
And like snakes with poisoned fangs
Lead to danger and to death!
Fickle fortune, ever fleeting,
Loves not with a lasting love;
Only fools her favours seek,
Strange the motives, mortals move!
Fortune! if she spurned the fickle,
'Twere no stain upon her fame,—
But the worthless and the worthy
To the fickle maid are same!
Love! it is an emptier sound,
Ending in delusion, pain!
Sad bereavement, death and loss
Rend the heart of luckless men.
When we meet the loved and true
Solitude as peopled seems;
Penury hath charms to please,
Sorrow is like happy dream!
When we lose the loved and true,
Pleasures mock us and delude;

Life is like a poisoned dart,
Company is solitude! (28)

"Thus each fleeting earthly object
Ends in sorrow, ends in grief;—
Charity alone endureth,
Unto others bring relief!
And our life is vain and fleeting,
Fortune's fickle favours fly;
Righteousness alone endureth,
Turn not from the righteous way!
Stain not, youth, these holy rites,
Do them not with lust of war;
Seek salvation's stainless bliss,—
Than war's glory mightier far!
Conquer lust and vain desires,—
Born with mortals at their birth,—
Conquest of thyself, good youth,
Is the conquest of the earth!
Weak are they and narrow-hearted,
Earthly power who seek to wield;
Slaves of passions, slaves of impulse,
Even like cattle in the field!
Joys that pleased thee yesterday,
In thy memory dwell alone!
Pleasures are but fleeting dreams,
Be not thou to pleasures prone!
Ever wished, but still deceiving,
Cherished but to cause us woe,
Never present,—never leaving,—
Earthly joy—our greatest foe!

In this holy mountain range,
   Where the Gangâ wanders far,
Work thy own salvation, youth!
   Leave, O leave this lust of war." (36)

Thus the mighty god, disguised,
   Spoke to Arjun,—paused awhile;
And in humble words but strong,
   Arjun answered with a smile. (37)

"Full of weight and wisdom, father,
   Are the peaceful words I hear;
Full of import and suggestion
   Is thy utterance, deep yet clear.
Like an independent Sâstra
   In its reasons strong in sooth,
Like the ancient holy Vedas
   Mighty in its force and truth!
Inviolate in its ample force,
   Like the vast inviolate seas;
Gentle in its wealth of sense,
   Like a hermit's soul of peace!
Who could utter thoughts so noble
   Save a great and noble heart,—
Words emphatic, peaceful, clear,
   Void of quibble, void of art!
But perchance to thee unknown
   The object of my holy rites,
Hence in accents sweet and peaceful
   Speakest thou of anchorites.

E'en the god of speech will err
When he speaks of things unknown;
E'en the noblest efforts fail
Against inviolate rules when done! (43)

"Father! thy advice is holy,
But, alas, it suits not me,
As the starry sky of midnight
Doth not suit the light of day!
I am of the Kshatriya race,
Pandu's son, of Prithâ born;
Serve the mandates of my elder,
By his foes of glory shorn.
I these holy rites perform
Obedient to great Vyâsa's word;
Toiling still in ceaseless penance
For great Indra, mighty lord! (46)

"Oh! woeful are decrees of fate,
And mortals' bliss is often crossed!
His kingdom, brothers, and his wife
Our elder staked on dice and lost!
And now in evenings long and drear,
My brothers grieving at their fate,
With proud Draupadî great of heart,
The term of my devotions wait.
They tore the garments from our backs,
And shamed us in the palace hall;
They pierced our hearts,—our foemen vile,—
With bitter taunts upon our fall.

And in the presence of the chiefs
They dragged Draupadî chaste and true!
Death sealed in her disgrace a vow
Of vengeance on our impious foe!
Behind Duhsâsan,—impious chief!—
Appeared Draupadî,—great in mind,
Even as the shadow of a tall tree
Is at sunset cast behind.
'In vain I look upon my lords,
Untrue to duty and to me,'—
Such bitter thoughts her bosom rent,
And checked the tear-drop in her eye!
Our virtuous elder bore unmoved
The insult dire, the blow unkind!
Oh! what is conquest over foemen
To such conquest of one's mind?
For noble hearts retain their peace
Albeit by grief and passions riven;
The ocean steps not o'er its bounds
Albeit by mighty tempests driven!
'Twas friendship with our impious cousins
Which unto this shame hath led,—
Bitter is his untimely end
Neath falling banks who sits for shade.
Men who fear nor sin nor shame,
Right and wrong who do not see,—
Who can compass their designs?
Who can fathom fate's decree? (56)

"Disgraced, insulted by our foe,
My heart, my heart had ceased to beat,

If in this strong and vengeful arm
  I hoped not retribution great!
Disgraced, insulted by our foes,—
  Low, low, as cattle on the plain,
We shame to see each other's face,
  Nor show our face to other men!
Humbled by the loss of glory,
  Humbled by disgrace, alas!
Mortals, when bereft of honour,
  Are like low and trodden grass! (59)

"But look aloft! Yon mighty peaks
  By living beings are not crossed!
Loftiness is virtue rare,
  Honour is a mortal's boast!
Fickle Fortune smiles upon us,
  True and constant is our fame,
And the name of man befits us,
  While high honour decks our name!
Highest in the rolls of honour!—
  He is worthy of his fame;
And the finger of the counter
  Pointeth not to worthier name!
Even this lofty towering range
  Might be crossed by living wight,
But the man of worth and honour
  Is inviolate in his might!
Glory on their race they bring,
  Glory on the earth they spread,
Whose effulgent stainless honour
  Casts the moonbeams in the shade!

And their wrath like lurid lightning
  Cowering foemen soon will pierce;
And their name in glory's records
  Stands in pride through untold years! (65)

"I seek not joys, I seek not wealth,
  Fleeting as the water's race,
Nor trembling for the fear of death,
  Seek I Brahmâ's holy grace!
But I seek to wash the stain,—
  Stain for which this heart hath bled,—
With the tear-drops for our foes,
  By their sorrowing widows shed!
If the hope on which I've rested
  Be unreal, idle, vain,
Be it so! Thy words are wasted,
  Pardon if I cause thee pain!
Till I conquer,—crush my foes,
  Win again our long-lost fame,
Salvation's self to me were vain,—
  Hindrance to my lofty aim!
For the man is yet unborn,
  Or is dead like trodden grass,
Who will let his good sword sleep,
  Tamely let his glory pass!
Whose warm blood moves not in ire,—
  The conquered loon,—the crouching slave,—
Dost thou, holy anchorite,
  Call him man,—that abject knave?
Beshrew the title of a man,
  Void of worth and manlike pride;

Welcome is that honoured name
 Graced by worth and manlike deed!
He whose name in wonder spoken
 Pales the name of other men,
He whose deeds are known to foemen,
 He is MAN among all men! (73)

"Yet more! Our good, long-suffering elder
 Vows revenge against the foe,—
Awaits my help, as thirsty travellers
 Wait the cooling draught in woe.
Unmindful of his elder's hest,
 Unmindful of his elder's bliss,
The man who shirks his task in trouble,
 Is a traitor to his race!
And wherefore preachest to me, father!
 Life retired before my time,
The ancients forest-life prescribed
 Not in our youth but after prime.
My mother, living in the woods,
 My brothers in misfortunes dire,
My duty, as by Vyâsa told,
 Forbid me, father, to retire!
And honour's maxims, holy saint,
 Forbid the noble and the true
To seek for safety in retirement
 From a great and conquering foe!
Then let me, father! on these hills
 Like clouds of autumn waste away!
Or pleasing Indra, mighty monarch,—
 Wipe our shame in battle's fray!"

Arjun spoke, and gracious Indra
  Stood in heavenly form and might,
Clasped the young and pious hero,
  Bade him worship Siva great! (80)

"To Siva, mighty god, thy worship pay,
For he alone can help thee in the fray,
And thou shalt be unconquered in thy might;"
Thus Indra spoke, and vanished from his sight. (81)

BOOK IX.

THE ADVENT OF SIVA.

By Indra's mandate Arjun great
  Once more began his pious rites,
And worship paid to saintly Siva
  Dwelling in far Kailâsa's heights.
Firm in his purpose, pure in heart,
  Unwearied in the sun's hot ray,
In rigid fasts, in penance long
  The pious chief passed many a day.
Mortifying flesh and sense,
  In penance long he passed his hours,
In pious rites, unmoved as rock,
  For high resolve hath wondrous power!
Luscious fruits that ripened near him,
  Crystal rills that rippled by,—
For righteous is sweetest nectar,—
  Drew from him nor wish nor sigh!
He boasted not, he ne'er despaired,
  He never ceased from righteous toil,
Nor wrath nor passions in his heart
  His noble steadfast faith could soil.
He wore a world subduing power,
  Though pale with many a rigid rite,

And saints beheld him with a fear,—
 The great in heart are great in might! (6)

Brighter than the nightly fires
 His radiance seemed the woods to fill,
More mighty than the boundless sea,
 And loftier than the towering hill:
His sacred *mantras* ever chanting,
 With a beauteous light he shone;
And on his features fell a radiance
 Like the halo of the sun!
Clad in armour dark, he wore
 His mighty bow across his chest;
So wears the lofty wood-clad hill
 The glorious rainbow on his breast!
When for ablutions,—fixed by rules,—
 He walked betimes, in morning's hour,
The mountain felt his mighty tread,
 For worth is might and worth is power!
A wondrous lustre on him shone
 When Arjun stood serene and high,—
It shone across the firmament,
 And flashed upon the upper sky!
And on moonless nights there fell
 Upon the prince a wondrous ray,—
And like the silver beams of moon
 It pierced the darkness of the sky!
So bright, so clear the light celestial
 That the paléd orb of sun
Marching through the cloudless sky
 Scarce with wonted radiance shone! (13)

Holy hermits viewed in awe
His crimson locks, his bow unbent!
They whispered,—"Is it Siva's self
On mighty Asur's death intent?
Is he great Indra or the Sun?
Or Fire, who helps our pious rites?
No mortal he of woman born,
Such glory decks no anchorites."
But unlike the tongues of Fire
Serene was Arjun's radiant light;
Unlike the scorching rays of Sun,
'Twas gentle in its wondrous might!
As virtues seek true gentleness,
As moral rules seek peaceful thought,
As righteous laws seek precepts pure,
The troubled saints great Siva sought! (17)

Dazzled, blinded, when they came,
By Siva's more than solar light,
They sought in vain with mortal eyes
To compass Siva's glorious might!
In humble prayer they sought the Lord
Of times to come and times gone by,—
And by its grace they faintly saw
His glorious mien, his triple eye!
Resting on his sacred bull,
His glorious arm of wondrous might,
Sweet Umâ's lord, to Umâ dear,
Stood forth upon the mountain's height!
Far distant from the living world
He stood upon a snowy height;

But rock and ocean, earth and heaven
  Felt his presence and his might!
Coiling serpents stretched their length
  Around the muscles of his feet,
As on the vast and boundless earth
  High mountain ranges spread their height!
And on his blue and ample neck
  Great coiling serpents, white as snow,—
Even like the thread of twice-born mortals,—
  Caught its dark and tremulous glow!
By his tresses partly hid,
  Like Gangâ's ripples looked the moon,
And on his fair and ample forehead
  With a gentle radiance shone!
Permission gained, the holy saints
  Addressed the God with many a prayer,
Told him how a mortal's penance
  Filled the earth with mighty fear. (25)

"Mighty Lord of all the worlds!
  A mortal wielding Vritra's might,
Unceasing penances performs,
  The sun obscuring by his light!
A bow he wears and mighty quivers,
  Armour and a wondrous blade,
And plaited locks and skin and barks,—
  A saint! in arms accoutred dread!
Earth trembles 'neath his mighty tread,
  And when he prays at evening's glow,
The starry skies are hushed to peace,
  The evening breezes cease to blow!

His force terrific could subdue
  This world with Gods and Asurs brave!
What mighty task, what daring feat
  His matchless strength might not achieve!
Or if he seeks to rule the world,—
  Or to destroy in wantonness,—
Or to attain salvation pure,
  Great Lord of hosts! we may not guess!
Thou knowest all, O mighty Lord!
  World hides no secret from thine eye!
Thou knowest all, and thou canst save,
  And we are safe when thou art nigh!" (31)

Unto them great Siva spoke
  In accents deep and full of grace,
Deep as the troubled ocean's roar
  Resounding to the ends of space! (32)

"Know ye, who with lofty rites
  Worships in Badrika's heath?
Earth-born man,—but part of Him,
  Who is life and who is death!
Lofty penance he performs
  Foes to conquer and to quell,
Foes who rule this boundless earth
  Indra's mighty power assail!
By the will of Lotus-Born,
  Krishna and great Arjun came,—
Sons of men by mortals bred,—
  Men to save in Brahmâ's name! (35)

"But the wily Asur,—Muka—
  Dreaded by the gods in sky,
Seeks to kill the mighty Arjun ;—
  I must to his safety hie.
But to conquer mighty Arjun
  Openly 'twere vain to try ;
Muka takes the form of wild-boar
  To achieve his purpose sly!
I will take the form of hunter,
  Pierce the wild-boar in the heart,
Claiming honour of the wild sport,
  Arjun too will send his dart!
Pale with rigid rites and penance,
  Still he wields a wondrous might,
Ere the mortal wins my favour
  He must prove his worth in fight!" (39)

Thus speaking to the holy saints
  A forester in guise he went!
His ample chest bedewed with toil,
  With many a pearl and sandal paint!
With flowering tendrils rudely tied
  His clustering manly locks he wore,
And bright a peacock's painted feather
  O'er his bloodshot eyes he bore!
A mighty bow with arrows keen
  He carried in his brawny hand,—
And like a rain-cloud dark he looked,
  The leader of a forest band!
And all his hosts in various guise,
  Obedient to their Master's word,

Assembled like a hunting troop,
 With bow and arrow, lance and sword!
They parcelled out the mountain wood,
 Obedient to their Leader's will,
Shaking the earth with mighty sound,
 Forward marched the hunters still! (44)

Screams and sounds of birds and beasts
 Filled far and near the forest land,
As if the woods and mountains quaked
 In terror of that hunter-band!
And the flying beasts and birds
 Forgot awhile their mutual strife;
A common danger made them comrades,
 And a common fear of life!
The timid Chamari * feign would fly,
 Bewildered by the hunter's yell,—
But in the jungles wild and thick
 Was caught his white and bushy tail.
The mighty lion, forest-king,
 Owned in his heart no dastard fear!
He calmly viewed the hunters pass,
 Through echoing woods, through gorges drear!
The fish leap out from jungle lake,
 The wild beasts on its margin crowd,
And tall trees by the tuskers broken
 With their juice its waters cloud.
Buffaloes tearing through the forest
 Broke in twain the tangled trees,

* The yak of the Himalayas, from whose bushy white tails fans are made.

And many a wild flower, tossed and shaken,
  With their fragrance filled the breeze!
Wild beasts, splashing through the water,
  Felled the plantains, crushed the grain,
Dashed aside the water-lily,
  Like a summer storm and rain!
Sweeping thus through forest lands
  At length the hunters came and stood,
Where grazed in peace the gentle deer,
  Nor dreaded harm,—in Arjun's wood!
And Siva marked,—black as a cloud,—
  A wild boar in the covert rise;
Tearing the earth with angry tusks,
  It flew,—the Asur in disguise! (53)

Leaving his hosts behind the forest lake,
Concealed by creepers and by jungle-brake,
The Lord of hosts, resistless in his force,
Tracked the mighty wild boar in its course. (54)

BOOK X.

THE BOAR HUNT.

THE Boar with wondrous strength endowed
In its deep tusks and mighty jaw,—
As if to tear the firm set rocks,—
With glaring eyes great Arjun saw!
"Uprooting trees with his great tusks,
And piercing rocks with dreadful might,
He comes at me,"—thus Arjun thought,—
"As if to challenge me to fight!
Beasts of prey forget their strife
In this my peaceful hermitage,
Wherefore then on death intent
Intrudes this wild boar in its rage?
Was he my foe in previous life?
Does cherished hatred speed him still?
Despising every living creature
Death to me he seeks to deal!
Much my doubting heart misgives,—
No beast,—he is a deadly foe!
Spontaneously a friend or foe
The instincts of our nature know!" (5)

Pondering thus he took his bow,
Fit emblem of his matchless might.

And on it quickly placed his arrow,
Ever true in many a fight!
Admiring Siva marked his mien,
His circling bow, his stately height,—
"The mortal stands, as once I stood,
And slew Tripurâ in my might!"
And Siva bent his sounding bow,
The mountain sank beneath his tread!
And the snake that formed the bowstring
Shot forth sparks, all flaming red!
Frightened tuskers fled the sound
Of Siva's bow, terrific, high,
As lightning from rain-cloud falls,
The arrow shot across the sky!
The Boar's tough hide, like seasoned Tamâl,
Pierced the dart like flakes of snow!
Unchecked, in earth it disappeared
As sharks in water sink below!
That instant as the lightning's radiance
Shortening distance, as by spell,
And quick as thought, great Arjun's arrow
On the mighty wild boar fell!
Red in hot blood fell the Boar,
Tearing rocks in rage and pride;
Glared at Arjun in its anger,
Groaned in agony, and died. (12)

Though rich in darts, great Arjun sought
The shaft the mighty prize had won;
For noble hearts are grateful ever,
And remember service done!

He saw a hunter near the beast,
A bow across his ample chest,—
A messenger who came to tell
His mighty Leader's high behest! (14)

"Thy gentle mien thy worth proclaims,
These rites proclaim thy holy peace,
And aye, thy lofty presence speaketh
Of a glorious god-like race!
Thy glory shames the sun's bright ray,
Thy mighty power is known to men,
Then wherefore takest thou this dart
With which our Chief this boar hath slain?
Or perchance our Leader's arrow
To thy arrow is akin,
And unconscious thou proceedest,
Erring, into paths of sin!
But not alone 'tis base to steal
Another's arrow from the field,
A chief like thee might blush to send
His shaft on game by others killed!
Or if, in sooth, thou seek'st this dart,
Come, ask our Leader openly;
Mighty Ruler!—he will yield
His dart to gain a friend like thee!
Unto our kind and gracious Chief
A humble prayer is never lost,
He knows the pain the lowly suffer,
When their humble prayer is crossed.
Or hast thou with a Brâhman's folly
On dead beast thy arrow driven?

Ignorance doth cover sin,
Our Chief thy folly hath forgiven!
Beshrew such folly, honest friend!
Depart in peace, nor sin again,
For who will pardon frequent sins,—
Incessant winds stir up the main!
My Chief forgives this foolish act,
Nor seeks to cause a hermit pain;
Come, yield this arrow to our Lord,
And from him wealth and grace obtain!
Yonder, by that lofty tree,
Stands he,—our Chief, thou mark'st him plain,
Obey his will, his favours seek,
And thou shalt all thy wish obtain!" (24)

Like a rock by surges beaten,
Angered by this bitter taunt,
Arjun still thus gently answered,
Great in patience and restraint! (25)

"Well skilled in words! Why seek'st thou not
To turn thy master from this strife?
Knowest thou not that menials perish
When their chief surrenders life?
Thy Leader's arrow may have gone
Among yon rugged rocks astray;—
Nor insult thus an anchorite,
For pride to ruin leads the way!
Many a bright and piercing arrow
In my ample quiver lies;

I value not celestial darts,
And scarce a mountaineer's would prize!
Beasts range the wood, to none belong,
Whoever kills them takes the game;
Then let thy Chief his pride forego,
And peacefully forego his claim.
You counselled me to beg the dart
As favour from your Chief in peace;
To win by prowess, not to ask,
Is the proud custom of my race.
You counselled friendship;—Kshatriya I,—
And he a hunter in this range!
Mighty tuskers scarce would seek
In skulking jackals friendship strange!
You counselled me to court his grace,
Presumptuous words!—I pardon free;
Then let thy Chief give up this shaft,
Nor seek with taunts to anger me!" (32)

Thus unto the hunter wild
Arjun spoke in angry mood,
And the forest messenger
Went where mighty Siva stood!
And the ample chested Chief,
With the bow across his breast,
Stood against the lofty sky,
Seemed the Lord of all the host!
Stood before him warlike Arjun,
Pale with penances, but proud,
Swelling with a mighty passion,
Like a fire in smoky shroud!

Resting on his mighty bow,
  Calm in strength, and patiently,
Mighty in his matchless power,
  Like the calm inviolate sea!
With a more than mortal form,
  Dark in hue, of stately size,
Like the world-protecting Vishnu,
  Hidden in a mortal's guise! (37)

Saintly in his penance and his rite,
Glorious in his prowess and his might!
To him the Lord of arméd hunters came,
As comes the dark cloud with the lightning's gleam! (38)

BOOK XI.

THE COMBAT.

TOWERING like a forest tree
  Stood the God of the lofty mind,
And his darksome hosts remained
  Like his shadow cast behind.
And against the warlike Arjun
  Siva shook his sounding bow,—
And the mountains seemed to split,
  And the skies re-echoed low!
Arjun shot his countless arrows
  With his more than mortal skill,—
But by Siva's shafts averted
  Arjun's arrows useless fell! *
Thick and fast across the sky
  Siva's wingéd arrows fly,
And with a lurid lustre shine,—
  Like the lightning's lurid ray!
Speeding through great Arjun's shafts,
  On that warlike chief they fell,
But the haughty warrior stood
  Dauntless and unshaken still!

* Hindu poets are fond of conceiving that great warriors can avert the enemy's arrow by their own in mid-air.

Still he proudly stood and fought,—
Vain his skill and vain his ire!
For his weapons shattered fell,
And his eyes flashed angry fire!
Wondering at the hunter's skill,
Arjun, conqueror of his foes,
Paused in silence and in doubt,—
In his heart these thoughts arose. (7,

"Warriors great of matchless power
I have met and beaten all!
Doth the sun bow to the moon?
Before the swain will Arjun fall?
Is this all magic, is this dream?
Or am I mighty Arjun still?
Why conquers not my matchless power
This mountaineer's untutored skill?
Rending the sky as if in twain,
Shaking the wide earth's solid frame,
How fights this boorish mountaineer!
Such deeds a man disguised proclaim!
Not Bhîshma's self nor Drona owns
Such skill to shield, to send the dart!
And can a simple mountain swain
Possess such superhuman art?
Whoe'er he be, his mighty power
By *shafts celestial* * I will quell!

* The *celestial shaft* is another favourite conception of Hindu poets Such shafts are supposed to have the power of creating darkness and light, fire and rains, snakes and eagles, &c., as described below. The idea is similar to the Greek idea of Apollo's sending his shafts to create a plague or some other calamity.

Nor shall a forest hunter's skill
'Gainst Arjun's matchless art prevail!" (12)

Pondering thus he quickly sent
Mighty shaft of death-like sleep;—
And a shadow filled the sky,
And the gloom of midnight deep!
Faint and powerless Siva's forces
Fell into a death-like sleep,
As a flippant youthful speaker
Falls abashed when questioned deep!
But the spreading gloom dispelling,
Siva sent a radiance bright,—
And as learning gloom dispelleth,—
Waked his hosts to new-born light!
Sorrowing Arjun thus beheld
His weapon lost and vain his art!
Fired with wrath the hero sent
The shaft of snakes,—a dreaded dart!
Pouring from their poisonous tongues
Liquid fire like lightning bright,
Countless myriad winged serpents
In the blue vault took their flight!
With their hue of molten gold
Reddening all the livid sky,
Flew the snakes across the view,
As the flashing meteors fly!
But unnumbered golden eagles
Issued from great Siva's dart!
And the serpents fled those birds,
Vain again was Arjun's art!

Burning with a mighty anger
  At the hunter's skill, he sped
A flaming shaft of fatal force,
  The shaft of fire, not fuel-fed!
With a sound like bursting rocks,
  Hiding the sun with flashes dire,
Casting crimson sparks around,
  Terrific rose the mighty fire!
Towering high like mountain peaks,
  Like molten gold, before, behind,
Flaming like the Kinsuk flower
  Spread the fire before the wind!
Rolled the red fire's tongues of flame,
  As on the world's destruction bent!
Siva quelled the mighty flame
  By the shaft of clouds he sent.
Quick and bright the lightning gleamed,
  And the rain-clouds, mountain high,
Deep incessant torrents poured
  Like Gangâ pouring from the sky!
The fire was quenched, but Arjun still
  Sent other shafts of wondrous might;
But vain his efforts,—vain our toil,
  When struggling 'gainst an adverse fate! (25)

Long waged the fierce and mighty war,
  Till Siva, pleased with Arjun's might,
Withdrew all shafts from Arjun's quivers,
  Ended thus the unequal fight!
And aye withdrew from Arjun's mien
  His armour streaked with rays of gold,

So from the sun the wind withdraws
The lightning clouds in many a fold.
Like shining blade from scabbard drawn,
Like cobra darting from his skin,
Or like the tusker wild and furious,
Breaking from his cord and chain,
Or like the lion, with wild roar
Springing from his desert cave,
Or like the flame which leaps from smoke,
All armour-less, shone Arjun brave!
Undaunted chief! He little recked
His person streaked with purple blood!
Forward he leaped with angry shout,
And shook the hills beneath his tread!
And with his bow, like Indra's lightning,
Wielding it with all his might,
He struck his foe, as strikes a tusker
At some tree of ancient height!
But vain the effort, vain the toil,
The shattered weapon useless flew;—
Last refuge of his dauntless pride,
His mighty sword at last he drew! (32)

Shielding self from Siva's darts,
Marching forward bold and free,
Arjun came with measured step,
Glorious as the sunlit sea!
But the good and trusty falchion
By great Siva's arrows driven,
Broke and fell with sound of thunder,
As from clouds the bolt of heaven!

Reft of bow and shining blade,
  Reft of armour golden bright,
Like the monster of the sea,
  Darted Arjun in his might! (35)

Viewing Arjun reft of weapons,
  Siva cast his arms aside,
Hand to hand the warriors wrestle
  Like two tuskers in their pride!
And the sound of mutual blows,
  The hunter and the hero gave,
Like the sound of bursting rocks,
  Was echoed from the mountain cave!
And the blows which Siva dealt
  Left their impress on the chief!
Proudly Arjun bore the wounds,
  Felt no pain and felt no grief!
But the blows which Arjun gave
  Were beaten back from Siva's chest,
As the surges of the ocean
  From the mountain's rocky breast!
Reeling from the hunter's blows,
  Charging with a mighty rage,
Arjun grasped him in his arms,
  In close fight the chiefs engage!
With their arms and with their feet
  They tug and strain and wrestle still,
And beneath their mighty tread
  Shakes the everlasting hill!
Siva's hosts bewildered view
  The wondrous fight,—with terror faint!

Who's above and who below?
  Is that Siva or the saint?
Freed at last from mutual grasp,
  Sounding their arms they spring in air!
The bank gives way beneath their tread,
  And falls into the streamlet fair!
Siva springs into the air,
  Arjun pulls him by the feet,
And to throw him on the ground,
  Holds them close with all his might. (44)

Mercy moves the heart of Sambhu great,
For pious Arjun holds him by the feet!
The god relents,—his heart is full of grace,
He holds the hero in a dear embrace! (45)

BOOK XII.

PRAYER AND BLESSING.

WITH wonder struck the hero views
  The Lord of hosts in ashes smeared ;
He views the crescent in his locks,
  And bows before the God revered !
His arrows and his mighty bow
  Appear once more before his sight !
Himself he finds in armour clad,
  And in its case the falchion bright !
Clouds pour forth a gentle rain,
  Skies send heavenly blossoms fair,
And a gentle heavenly music
  Floats upon the fragrant air !
And the gods by Indra bidden
  Gather in their realm on high,
And their chariots gem-bespangled
  Are like bright stars in the sky !
Heavenly swans with tinkling bells,
  Attendants on the gods on high,
With their softly waving plumage
  Gently sail across the sky !
His purpose done, his wish obtained,
  Low, low, his forehead Arjun laid,
And unto the God of gods
  Thus in humble accents prayed. (6)

1.

" The world's Asylum! Lord of grace!
Whom men by worship may attain,
Saints by Thy grace have conquered death,
And showed the path to gods and men!

2.

" Who seeks Thee not in loving worship
Is a prey to sin and death!
A prey to fleeting world's illusions,
Mortals shun his hated breath!

3.

" Who seeks Thee with a loving worship,
Shunning world's deceitful ways,
He finds in Thee his true salvation,
Lord of Mercy! 'Tis Thy grace!

4.

" Some seek for pleasures on this earth,
Some strive for heavenly joys and bliss,
But holy refuge there is none
Save Thee! O Lord of holiness!

5.

" Who seeks Thee, finds his haven shore,
Who shuns Thee, walks the downward path,
For this is Law! 'Tis not Thy anger,
Thou art Mercy, void of wrath!

6.

"*We love Thee with a tainted love,*
Thy form of grace we may not know,
But even thus Thy worship, Lord!
Salvation brings to us below.

7.

"*Illusions mock our mortal eyes,*
Our actions like a shadow flee!
Who views but Thee beholds the truth,
His acts are true who trusts in Thee!

8.

"*Saintly teachers on this earth*
They teach us precepts good and great;
Thou alone, with mighty grace,
From earthly bonds can liberate!

9.

"*To liberate this troubled earth*
From sin's tornado, passion's storm,
Thou wearest forms unto our eyes,—
For Thou art Mercy,—void of form!

10.

"*Thou art death and Thou art life,*
The universe lives in Thy laws;
Thou salvation of the pure,
Of mighty causes Thou FIRST CAUSE!"

Thus the good and pious Arjun
  Did great Sambhu's blessings crave;
Sambhu to the pious hero
  Heavenly arms and blessings gave.
And the lore by Siva given,
  Radiant with a crimson flame,
As the sun unto a rain-cloud,
  So unto great Arjun came!
Indra and the gods assembled,
  Blessed the man of steadfast faith;
Gave unto him arms celestial,
  Showed him glory's lofty path! (19)

"Faithful mortal! be thy wish fulfilled!"
Thus Siva spoke, and strength and faith instilled;
And Arjun came once more to Dvaita's wood,
And reverent bowed to Yudhishthir the good. (20)

APPENDIX TO THE HUNTER AND THE HERO.

In the Translation.		*In the Original Poem.*	
Books I. to VI.		Books I. to VI.	
	ver.		ver.
Book VII.	... 1	Book VII.	... 1
,,	... 2	,,	... 2
,,	... 3	,,	... 3
,,	... 4	,,	... 4
,,	... 5	,,	... 9
,,	... 6	,,	... 10
,,	... 7	,,	... 19
,,	... 8	,,	... 28
,,	... 9	Book VIII.	... 4
,,	... 10	,,	... 5
,,	... 11	,,	... 9
,,	... 12	,,	... 10
,,	... 13	,,	... 11
,,	... 14	,,	... 13
,,	... 15	,,	... 15
,,	... 16	,,	... 16
,,	... 17	,,	... 19
,,	... 18	,,	... 22
,,	... 19	,,	23, 24
,,	... 20	,,	25, 26
,,	... 21	,,	... 27
,,	... 22	,,	... 33
,,	... 23	,,	35, 36
,,	... 24	,,	49, 51
,,	... 25	,,	... 56
,,	... 26	Book IX.	... 16
,,	... 27	,,	... 17
,,	... 28	,,	... 19
,,	... 29	,,	... 23
,,	... 30	,,	... 24
,,	... 31	Book X.	... 1
,,	... 32	,,	... 4
,,	... 33	,,	... 10
,,	... 34	,,	... 11
,,	... 35	,,	... 14
,,	... 36	,,	... 15
,,	... 37	,,	... 18
,,	... 38	,,	... 20
,,	... 39	,,	... 22
,,	... 40	,,	... 23
,,	... 41	,,	... 30
,,	... 42	,,	... 34

In the Translation.		*In the Original Poem.*	
	ver.		ver.
Book VII.	... 43	Book X.	... 39
,,	... 44	,,	... 43
,,	... 45	,,	... 44
,,	... 46	,,	... 45
,,	... 47	,,	... 46
,,	... 48	,,	... 48
,,	... 49	,,	... 53
,,	... 50	,,	... 54
,,	... 51	,,	... 62
,,	... 52	,,	... 63
Book VIII.		Book XI.	
Book IX.		Book XII.	
Book X.	... 1	Book XIII.	1
,,	... 2	,,	... 3
,,	... 3	,,	... 4
,,	... 4	,,	... 5
,,	... 5	,,	... 6
,,	... 6	,,	... 14
,,	... 7	,,	... 17
,,	... 8	,,	... 18
,,	... 9	,,	... 20
,,	... 10	,,	... 24
,,	... 11	,,	... 27
,,	... 12	,,	... 31
,,	... 13	,,	... 32
,,	... 14	,,	... 35
,,	... 15	,,	... 37
,,	... 16	,,	... 41
,,	... 17	,,	... 45
,,	... 18	,,	... 46
,,	... 19	,,	... 59
,,	... 20	,,	... 60
,,	... 21	,,	... 63
,,	... 22	,,	... 66
,,	... 23	,,	... 68
,,	... 24	,,	70, 71
,,	... 25	Book XIV.	... 1
,,	... 26	,,	... 8
,,	... 27	,,	... 9
,,	... 28	,,	... 10
,,	... 29	,,	... 13
,,	... 30	,,	... 18
,,	... 31	,,	... 22

In the Translation.	ver.	*In the Original Poem.*	ver.
Book X.	32	Book XIV.	25
,,	33	,,	26
,,	34	,,	31
,,	35	,,	35
,,	36	,,	37
,,	37	,,	41
,,	38	,,	42
Book XI.	1	Book XV.	33
,,	2	,,	34
,,	3	,,	36
,,	4	,,	43
,,	5	,,	44
,,	6	,,	46
,,	7	Book XVI.	1
,,	8	,,	17
,,	9	,,	18
,,	10	,,	19
,,	11	,,	23
,,	12	,,	24
,,	13	,,	25
,,	14	,,	27
,,	15	,,	32
,,	16	,,	36
,,	17	,,	37
,,	18	,,	40
,,	19	,,	42
,,	20	,,	49
,,	21	,,	51
,,	22	,,	52
,,	23	,,	54
,,	24	,,	55
,,	25	,,	63
,,	26	Book XVII.	35
,,	27	,,	44
,,	28	,,	45
,,	29	,,	46
Book XI.	30	Book XVII.	50
,,	31	,,	51
,,	32	,,	52, 55
,,	33	,,	56
,,	34	,,	58
,,	35	,,	63
,,	36	Book XVIII.	1
,,	37	,,	2
,,	38	,,	3
,,	39	,,	5
,,	40	,,	6, 7
,,	41	,,	8
,,	42	,,	9
,,	43	,,	11
,,	44	,,	12
,,	45	,,	13
Book XII.	1	,,	15
,,	2	,,	16
,,	3	,,	17
,,	4	,,	18
,,	5	,,	19
,,	6	,,	21
,,	7	,,	22
,,	8	,,	23
,,	9	,,	24
,,	10	,,	25
,,	11	,,	26
,,	12	,,	27
,,	13	,,	28
,,	14	,,	29
,,	15	,,	30
,,	16	,,	35
,,	17	,,	44
,,	18	,,	45
,,	19	,,	46
,,	20	,,	48